Smoking Trends

ISSUES

KT-449-499

Volume 145

Editors: Cobi Smith and Sophie Crewdson

Independence

Educational Publishers
Cambridge

First published by Independence
PO Box 295
Cambridge CB1 3XP
England

British Library Cataloguing in Publication Data
Smoking trends. - (Issues ; 145)
1. Smoking
I. Smith, Cobi II. Crewdson, Sophie
362.2'96

ISBN-13: 9781861684110

Printed in Great Britain
MWL Print Group Ltd

Cover
The illustration on the front cover is by
Angelo Madrid.

CONTENTS

Chapter One: Smoking and Society

Chapter Two: Smoking and Health

Introduction

Smoking Trends is the one hundred and forty–fifth volume in the **Issues** series. The aim of this series is to offer up–to–date information about important issues in our world.

Smoking Trends looks at society's changing attitudes and regulations concerning tobacco use, as well as health issues associated with smoking.

The information comes from a wide variety of sources and includes:
Government reports and statistics
Newspaper reports and features
Magazine articles and surveys
Website material
Literature from lobby groups
and charitable organisations.

It is hoped that, as you read about the many aspects of the issues explored in this book, you will critically evaluate the information presented. It is important that you decide whether you are being presented with facts or opinions. Does the writer give a biased or an unbiased report? If an opinion is being expressed, do you agree with the writer?

Smoking Trends offers a useful starting–point for those who need convenient access to information about the many issues involved. However, it is only a starting–point. Following each article is a URL to the relevant organisation's website, which you may wish to visit for further information.

* * * * *

Smoking statistics

Information from ASH

Adults

⇨ Around 10 million adults smoke cigarettes in Great Britain. This is about a quarter of the population: 25% of men and 23% of women.

⇨ Smoking is highest among 20–24 year-olds: 34% of men and 30% of women smoke.

⇨ In 1974, 51% of men and 41% of women smoked cigarettes – nearly half the adult population.

⇨ Declines in smoking have been concentrated in older people. Almost as many young people still start smoking today but more established smokers are quitting.

Numbers who quit

⇨ 21% of women and 27% of men are now ex-smokers.

⇨ Surveys show that about 70% of current smokers would like to give up altogether.

Deaths from smoking

⇨ About half of all regular cigarette smokers will eventually be killed by their addiction.

⇨ Every year, around 114,000 smokers in the UK die from smoking-related causes.

Tobacco smoke contains:

⇨ Over 4,000 chemical compounds, present as either gases or as tiny particles.

⇨ These include carbon monoxide, arsenic, formaldehyde, cyanide, benzene, toluene and acrolein.

Young people

⇨ Over 80% of smokers start as teenagers.

⇨ In the United Kingdom about 450 children start smoking every day.

⇨ In England one-fifth of 15-year-olds are regular smokers: 16% of boys and 25% of girls.

⇨ It is illegal to sell cigarettes to children aged under 16.

Regional smoking rates

⇨ Smoking rates vary in different parts of the country (defined by the Government Office of the Regions).

⇨ In London and the South East 22% of adults smoke; in the North East the rate is 29%. In England overall 24% of people smoke.

⇨ In Scotland 27% of the population smoke.

⇨ In Wales the rate is 22%.

Socioeconomic differences

⇨ Smoking rates are markedly higher among poorer people

⇨ In 2005, 16% of men in higher managerial occupations smoked, compared with 34% in routine occupations.

Government revenue and expenditure

⇨ Earned £8,000 million in revenue from tobacco duty (ex VAT) in 2005–06.

⇨ Spent £23m on education campaigns.

⇨ Spent £52m to help people stop smoking.

⇨ This information is reprinted with permission from ASH (Action on Smoking and Health). Visit www.ash.org.uk for more information.

© ASH 2007

Young people and smoking

Information from ASH

Smoking prevalence

Children become aware of cigarettes at an early age. Three out of four children are aware of cigarettes before they reach the age of five whether or not the parents smoke.

The proportion of children who have experimented with smoking has fallen from 53% in 1982 to 39% in 2004. Experimentation is an important predictor of future use: a major US study revealed that 88% of adult smokers said they had started smoking by age 18.

Since 1993, girls have been more likely than boys to have ever smoked. This contrasts with the results of regional studies of children's smoking habits during the 1960s and 1970s which showed that more boys smoked than girls and that boys started earlier. In 1982, at ASH's instigation, the government commissioned the first national survey of smoking among children and found that 11% of 11–16 year-olds were smoking regularly.

During the early nineties prevalence remained stable at 10%, but by the mid nineties teenage smoking rates were on the increase, particularly among girls. Between 1996 and 1999, there was a decline in 11–15-year-olds smoking regularly. The reduction in smoking prevalence occurred mainly among 14–15-year-

action on smoking and health

olds. In 1998, the government set a target to reduce the prevalence of regular smoking among young people aged 11–15 from a baseline of 13% in 1996 to 11% by 2005 and 9% or less by 2010. Results from the 2006 survey show no change in smoking prevalence since 2003. As in previous years, girls are more likely to be regular smokers than boys. The proportion of regular smokers increases sharply with age: 1% of 11-year-olds smoke regularly compared with 20% of 15-year-olds.

What factors influence children to start smoking?

Children are more likely to smoke if one or both of their parents smoke and parents' approval or disapproval of the habit is also a critical factor.

A Dutch study revealed that adolescents with both parents smoking were four times more likely to be a smoker than their peers whose parents had never smoked. The same study also found that parental cessation whilst their children were young reduced the likelihood of adolescent smoking.

Numerous studies have shown that most young smokers are also influenced by their friends' and older siblings' smoking habits.

Other influences include tobacco advertising which fosters positive attitudes towards smoking and increases the likelihood of initiation. Some studies suggest that teenagers may also be influenced by viewing smoking in films.

Smoking and children's health

Children who smoke are two to six times more susceptible to coughs and increased phlegm, wheeziness and shortness of breath than those who do not smoke. Consequently, young smokers take more time off school than non-smokers. The earlier children become regular smokers and persist in the habit as adults, the greater the risk of developing lung cancer or heart disease.

Smokers are also less fit than non-smokers: the performance in a half marathon of a smoker of 20 cigarettes a day is that of a non-smoker 12 years older.

Passive smoking

Children are also more susceptible to the effects of passive smoking. Parental smoking is the main determinant of exposure in non-smoking children. Although levels of exposure in the home have declined in the UK in recent years, children living in the poorest households have the highest levels of exposure as measured by cotinine, a marker for nicotine.

Bronchitis, pneumonia, asthma and other chronic respiratory illnesses are significantly more common in infants and children who have one or two smoking parents.

Children of parents who smoke during the child's early life run a higher risk of cancer in adulthood and the larger the number of smokers in a household, the greater the cancer risk to non-smokers in the family. For a more detailed overview of the health impacts of passive smoking on children see the ASH briefing: *Passive smoking: the impact on children*.

Addiction

Children who experiment with cigarettes quickly become addicted to the nicotine in tobacco. A MORI survey of children aged 11 to 16 years found that teenagers have similar levels of nicotine dependence as adults, with one-third of those who smoke one or more cigarettes a week lighting up their first cigarette within 30 minutes of waking up and one in twelve lighting up within the first 5 minutes. In 2004, 66% of smokers aged 11–15 reported that they would find it difficult to go without smoking for a week while 79% thought they would find it difficult to give up altogether. One US study found that smoking just one cigarette in early childhood doubled the chance of a teenager becoming a regular smoker by the age of 17. During periods of abstinence, young people experience withdrawal symptoms similar to the kind experienced by adult smokers.

Smoking prevention

Since the 1970s, health education including information about the health effects of smoking has been included in the curricula of most primary and secondary schools in Great Britain. Research suggests that knowledge about smoking is a necessary component of anti-smoking campaigns but by itself does not affect smoking rates. It may, however, result in a postponement of initiation.

High prices can deter children from smoking, since young people do not possess a large disposable income. In Canada, when cigarette prices were raised dramatically in the 1980s and the early 1990s youth consumption of tobacco plummeted by 60%. An American study has shown that while price does not appear to affect initial experimentation of smoking, it is an important tool in reducing youth smoking once the habit has become established.

Children, smoking and the law

Since 1908, and currently under the Children and Young Persons (Protection from Tobacco) Act 1991, it has been illegal to sell any tobacco product to anyone below the age of 16. The Act increased the maximum fines for retailers found guilty of selling cigarettes to children to £2,500 and prohibited the sale of single cigarettes.

From 1 October 2007, the legal age for the purchase of tobacco in England and Wales will rise to 18. The amendment is designed to make it more difficult for young teenagers to obtain cigarettes, since, despite the law, children still succeed in buying

tobacco from shops and vending machines. In 2004, 66% of 11–15-year-old smokers reported that they bought their cigarettes from a shop, with older teenagers being much more likely to obtain their cigarettes from shops than younger children: 78% of 15-year-olds compared with 28% of those aged 11–12. During 2005 there were 89 prosecutions in England and Wales for underage tobacco sales, with 70 defendants being found guilty and 56 fined.

Legislation alone is not sufficient to prevent tobacco sales to minors. Both enforcement and community policies may improve compliance by retailers but the impact on underage smoking prevalence using these approaches alone may still be small. Successful efforts to limit underage access to tobacco require a combination of approaches that tackle the problem comprehensively.

⇨ This information is reprinted with permission from ASH (Action on Smoking and Health). Visit www.ash.org.uk for more information.

© ASH 2007

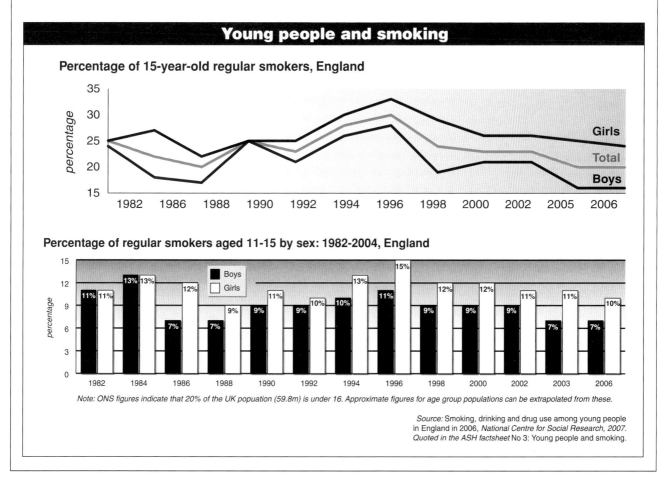

Young people and smoking

Percentage of 15-year-old regular smokers, England

Percentage of regular smokers aged 11-15 by sex: 1982-2004, England

Note: ONS figures indicate that 20% of the UK popuation (59.8m) is under 16. Approximate figures for age group populations can be extrapolated from these.

Source: Smoking, drinking and drug use among young people in England in 2006, *National Centre for Social Research, 2007. Quoted in the ASH factsheet* No 3: Young people and smoking.

Europe 'worst' for teen smoking

Information from Agence France Presse

Europe may be leading the effort to stamp out smoking in public places, but it has the highest incidence of teen smokers in the world, a study says.

Nearly 18% of Europeans aged 13 to 15 are smokers, more than twice the global average of 8.9%, according to the paper, published online on Friday by the British medical weekly *The Lancet*.

Next is the region of the Americas, with 17.5%, followed by Africa (9.2%), the Western Pacific (6.5%), the Eastern Mediterranean (5.0%) and Southeast Asia (4.3%).

When other tobacco use was factored in, such as chewing tobacco and snuff, the Americas came top with 22.2%, followed by Europe, with 19.8%; the global average was 17.3%.

The authors say they were surprised to see an apparently narrowing gap between boys and girls.

In the Americas, more girls smoke than boys, and there is only a small difference between the genders in Europe – 19.9% among boys, and 15.7% among girls.

Tobacco toll

In contrast, the smoking rate among boys is three times that among girls in the Western Pacific, a region that includes China, and the same applies to Southeast Asia.

Past calculations that the annual death toll from tobacco could double to 10 million by 2020 'may be a conservative estimate', said lead author Charles Warren of the United States Centres for Disease Control and Prevention (CDC).

'The true toll from tobacco use could be even greater, (given) high rates of non-cigarette tobacco use and high rates of smoking among young girls.'

The data come from questionnaires filled in by 747,000 students in 9,900 schools in 131 countries and the Gaza Strip and West Bank.

The students completed their questionnaires in the classroom, but confidentiality and anonymity were guaranteed, say the researchers.

The survey did however have some gaps in its coverage, namely a number of countries in western Europe as well as Australia, Canada, New Zealand and Japan.

⇨ This article was published on 17 February 2006 and is reprinted with permission from Agence France Presse. Visit www.afp.com for more information.

What's the effect of peer pressure on smoking?

Information from NHS Direct

Peer pressure is one of the most common reasons young people give for starting to smoke. Your peers are the group of people around the same age as you, often with the same interests as you, and who may go to your school or college.

You may feel you need to fit in with them by doing and liking the same things as everyone else. Sometimes this is to get into the in-crowd, or out of fear of being bullied.

You may feel pressure to wear certain clothes, or sometimes do

harmful things, such as smoking.

Not only is smoking bad for your health, it's also illegal for you to buy cigarettes if you're under 16. Smoking is against school rules, so you risk getting into trouble with your teachers. Many parents (including those who are smokers themselves) don't want their children to smoke, because they have seen the damage to their own health.

Some young people think these things make smoking even more exciting, but it is worth considering that if so many people don't want you

to smoke, there must be good reasons.

If your friends are putting you under pressure to smoke, even though you don't want to, think carefully whether they are the best people to hang around with. If they were really your friends they wouldn't bully you about smoking.

If you've only just started as a casual smoker, quit before you become part of the regular smoking crowd. You might even be able to get some of your friends to quit at the same time.

⇨ This article is reprinted with permission from NHS Direct. Visit www.nhsdirect.nhs.uk for more information.

Why the young smoke and how to stop them

Information from the Economic and Social Research Council

By the age of 16, some 32 per cent of girls and 16 per cent of boys are smokers. And, once started, the proportion of young people able to quit is minimal. Finding ways to help young people resist taking up smoking is clearly a high priority.

Now a new study undertaken at the Universities of Leeds and Staffordshire aims to do just that. By following a sample of young people over a six-year period from the ages of 11 to 18 years, researchers have identified not only young people's views about smoking but also some of the key predictors of starting to smoke.

'A key finding', explains researcher Professor Mark Conner, 'is that beliefs about smoking differ across both age and gender groups.' Hence, a broad-brush approach to helping young people resist smoking is less than effective.

'We suggest that interventions designed to reduce the numbers who take up smoking during adolescence need to be targeted by gender and age group,' Professor Conner argues.

Decisions by girls to take up smoking are strongly influenced by 'what others think of them'. Hence, believing that smoking is cool and will prove a source of status, popularity and social support at school is a strong predictor of which non-smoking girls will go on to become smokers. Interventions that stress the health problems associated with smoking cut little ice with girls. Rather, research suggests the need for interventions that help young women resist the perceived social pressure to smoke and reconceptualise smoking in order to downplay its perceived social benefits.

Non-smoking boys, on the other hand, may primarily be motivated by negative beliefs about smoking. So, stressing the health risks and cost of smoking may prove more

successful in helping boys resist the desire to start.

In terms of targeting messages at particular age groups, researchers find that younger smokers justify themselves in three ways: downplaying the health risks (i.e. it won't happen to me), extolling the 'benefits' (e.g. controlling stress), and viewing it as a temporary, youthful phenomenon (I'll give up when I'm older). Research suggests that health messages only have a significant impact on older children.

In general, findings indicate that any attempts to persuade children against smoking need to address both negative and 'positive' views on smoking. In other words, children may understand the 'negative' view that smoking can kill but still hold a 'positive' view that smoking calms your nerves. Interventions therefore need to point out why the 'positives' may not hold or can be achieved in other ways. For example, what other things can you do that would calm your nerves?

'We also clearly identified children's need to "justify" their decision to their peers not to smoke as an issue,' Professor Conner points out. 'For boys, an acceptable justification is the desire to be good at sport but this doesn't work among girls. We need to understand that children feel they need a good reason to say no and help them develop appropriate resistance skills.'

⇨ This information is reprinted with permission from the Economic and Social Research Council. Visit www.esrc.ac.uk for more information.

© 2004 Economic and Social Research Council

How images affect young people's own lifestyles

Information from the ESRC

Images young people see of those who smoke, drink or take drugs, have greater impact on their behaviour than anything others may say to them, according to new research sponsored by the ESRC.

These impressions can affect people without their being aware, says the study, led by Professor Paschal Sheeran of the University of Sheffield.

His report dismisses the idea that images found in advertising and the mass media, such as pictures of slim young women, have no influence on those who view them.

Some 450 secondary school-age pupils and 118 undergraduates took part in the research, which included surveys and carefully controlled experiments to examine whether, and how much, young people's own health choices are influenced by portrayals of smokers as 'cool' or drinkers as 'one of the lads'.

The findings provide valuable evidence for the Government and others anxious to reduce potentially unhealthy activities, particularly among the young.

According to the study, young people are generally not affected by what other people think, particularly when it comes to risk-taking pursuits such as smoking and drinking. If they decide to smoke, use drugs or, indeed, take healthy exercise, then probably they will go ahead and do so.

But in coming to that decision, they are more impressed by what others actually do, rather than what they say. For instance, they are more likely to drink if people they know are drinkers.

Professor Sheeran said: 'Young people have ideas about what the typical person who smokes, drinks, or exercises is like, and these images have an important effect on their own behaviour because they influence their decisions and willingness to do the same.

'Our experiments showed that in the same way that many people think that advertising affects others but not themselves, images can influence people, even though they don't believe this to be the case.'

Professor Sheeran added: 'The next time you're watching a TV programme, look to see how often someone is smoking or drinking, and how often you see someone taking physical exercise.

'Ask yourself what images are being presented. Is the drinker just an outgoing fun-loving girl? Is the exerciser a bit self-absorbed or out-of-the-ordinary? Do you think it matters how often these images are presented and whether they are likeable or dislikeable?'

In surveys of young people aged between 14 and 19, questions were asked about healthy

activities including exercise, sleep, and eating breakfast, as well as risky ones such as smoking, drinking and use of drugs. Researchers found that, regardless of their willingness or conscious intentions, young people were more likely to do a particular thing when they thought the image was positive and something they could identify with. This was true whether the activity was healthy or risky.

Computer-based tests for undergraduates included careful inclusion of words and images designed to suggest positive or neutral images of drinking alcohol, in what volunteers thought were actually language experiments.

Subsequent tests of how ready they were to drink revealed that whilst none believed they had been influenced in any way, they had.

The study points out that when it comes to smoking, young people may not intend indulging, but might be willing to do so under certain circumstances. However, it argues that just being willing to smoke affects whether they end up doing so, regardless of their intentions.

⇨ This information is reprinted with permission from the Economic and Social Research Council. Visit www.esrc.ac.uk for more information.

EU advertising ban

Information from biz/ed

An EU-wide ban on advertising tobacco products comes into force today. The ban will mean that firms will not be able to use any form of advertising to push their products using print, the Internet, TV and radio. The UK has extended the range of the ban and included advertising using clothing, hats and umbrellas. The ban has been agreed for some time but its implementation delayed to give tobacco firms and others affected by the ban time to adjust. In particular, a number of sports have been affected by the impending ban where tobacco sponsorship has been particularly high.

Yesterday's Hungarian grand prix was the last Formula 1 race in Europe to feature tobacco advertising although it is unclear how the law will operate when races are run outside the EU but televised in, for example, the UK. There has been a ban on tobacco advertising in the UK for Formula 1 since 2002.

The move is based on the assumption that there is a direct link between tobacco advertising and the take-up and continued use of tobacco in society as a whole. The tobacco firms argue that they are not seeking to advertise to encourage new smokers, especially the young, to take up smoking but to advertise their brand to existing smokers.

Supporters of the ban claim that tobacco firms rely on getting new customers as well as maintaining existing ones and as such they would not spend the massive amounts they do on advertising if it did not work in securing customers.

The UK Department of Health has welcomed the ban. It claims that a ban on advertising will cut the number of deaths by around 3,000 representing a fall of 2.5%. It claims that on average around 1.6 million people will see a billboard advertising tobacco every day and that the moves to ban tobacco advertising will help to finally break the link between advertising and smoking.

The tobacco companies will have to think of ways to market their products now that advertising is banned. In some respects, the fact that when you go into a newsagent, petrol station or supermarket there are walls of tobacco products staring you in the face may be one way but they might also consider more subtle ways of letting us know they are still around. Cars in Formula 1 for example could sport the colours of the tobacco firm that sponsors them without having the name on the vehicle. Tobacco advertising could be said to have been successful enough over the years for us all to recognise and associate these colours with the relevant firms.

⇨ The above information was published on 1 August 2005. It is reprinted with permission from biz/ed. Visit www.bized.co.uk for more information.

© 2005 biz/ed

Hollywood faces fury as smoking on screen returns to 1950s levels

By Chris Hastings

Their faces might light up the screen, but their actions are causing anti-smoking groups to fume. Some of Hollywood's biggest names, including Catherine Zeta-Jones, Nicole Kidman and Pierce Brosnan, are under fire after research showed that smoking on screen is at its highest for 50 years.

An analysis of 150 films produced between 1950 and 2002 has found that there are now about 11 depictions of smoking in every hour of the typical film.

The incidence of smoking, according to the study by scientists at the University of California, has risen steadily over the past decade and is higher than the corresponding figure for the 1950s, when films such as Alfred Hitchcock's *Rear Window* and *Vertigo* portrayed a highly glamorised image of cigarettes. The study also found that smoking scenes now feature in children's films.

The disclosure has infuriated anti-smoking campaigners who claim that films are encouraging the young to smoke. Some last night called for all films that depicted smoking to be given an 18 certificate.

Among the films analysed for the study were the James Bond film *Die Another Day*, *Star Wars: Attack of the Clones* and *Lord of the Rings: Fellowship of the Ring*.

Stanton Glantz, a professor at the School of Medicine at the University of California, who led the research, said that the prevalence of smoking in films was allowing manufacturers to overcome the difficulties created for them by restrictions on tobacco advertising.

'Films that feature cigarettes and smoking are worth millions to the tobacco companies in terms of advertising. This is particularly true

of a country like Britain where there is a strict ban on tobacco advertising,' he said.

'A dangerous habit that was once ignored by film-makers is now more high-profile than ever. This is particularly worrying in the light of research that shows that young people are taking up smoking because of what they see on the big screen.'

The study found that in films in the 1950s there was an average of 10.7 incidents of smoking per hour. Concerns about health and pressure from lobby groups saw this figure fall to 4.9 between 1980 and 1982, but by 2002, the total had risen to 10.9 depictions of smoking per hour.

As well as the films in the study, other box office hits, including Chicago, the Oscar-winning musical that starred Catherine Zeta-Jones and Renée Zellweger, *The Hours*, which starred Nicole Kidman, and

Monster, with Charlize Theron, have all featured characters who smoke.

Deborah Arnott, the director of Ash, the British anti–smoking organisation, said that it was referring the American findings to the British Board of Film Classification. She was particularly worried that children would be encouraged to smoke unless tougher restrictions were imposed on film content.

'I am not so concerned about seeing Charlize Theron smoking in a film like *Monster* because she is playing a psychotic lesbian and is not supposed to be a role model. It is a different story, however, when James Bond picks up a cigar in *Die Another Day*. He is very much a glamour figure.'

She added: 'I also do not understand why the hobbits have to smoke in *Lord of the Rings*. It would have been possible to leave those scenes out.'

> **'I don't think teenagers are going to smoke just because the hobbits are in *Lord of the Rings*. I think peer pressure, not cinema, is the defining factor here.'**

Simon Clark, the director of Forest, a pro-smoking campaign group, dismissed the concerns, saying that violence and gratuitous sex in films were far more damaging than the depiction of smoking.

'It's a nonsensical argument. It just shows you how po-faced and humourless these people can be,' he said. 'You can't impose an X-certificate on a film just because it has a shot of someone smoking. There is just no evidence to suggest young people start smoking because of what they see on screen.

'I don't think teenagers are going to smoke just because the hobbits are in *Lord of the Rings*. I think peer pressure, not cinema, is the defining factor here.'

A staff member at Eon films, which produces the James Bond films, said: 'It would be ridiculous if Bond did not smoke in the films. We try to keep the films as true to the original Ian Fleming novels as possible and he smokes quite a lot in them.

'Everyone knows Bond likes the finer things in life such as wine, food and fine cigars. Having him give up smoking would be like having him give up beautiful women.'

A spokesman for the British Board of Film Classification said that it was seeking opinions on whether smoking should affect a film's classification. There was no evidence yet, however, to suggest that young people were taking up smoking because of what they had seen on the big screen.

'All the evidence suggests that peer pressure is the major cause of young people smoking. This is fraught with difficulties. Should *101 Dalmations* carry an 18 certificate just because Cruella DeVil has a cigarette?'

The 1950s films in the study included *Touch of Evil*, with Orson Welles and Charlton Heston, *Peyton Place*, *A Star is Born*, with Judy Garland, and *Jailhouse Rock*, which starred Elvis Presley.

Many stars of the 1940s and 1950s regarded the cigarette as adding to their sexual allure. Some of Hollywood's biggest names such as Rita Hayworth in *Gilda* (1946), Joan Crawford, who famously lit up in *Mildred Pierce* (1945) and Humphrey Bogart, who chain–smoked through *The African Queen* (1951), regarded smoking as portraying a sense of sophistication, rebellion and sexual liberation.

⇨ This article first appeared in the Telegraph on 6 March 2004.

Smoking in movies linked to increase in global youth smoking

New research reveals how the incidence of smoking in US-made movies is influencing teenagers in countries far beyond American shores

Studies in Germany and Mexico, as well as further evidence from the United States, show a correlation between the amount of smoking imagery in films and the likelihood of young teenagers starting to smoke.

A report in the journal *Pediatrics* confirms that US films deliver billions of tobacco images to US children aged 10–14, the age group most likely to begin experimenting with cigarettes. The study found that three out of four movies (74%) studied contained smoking. By calculating the number of American

action on smoking and health

adolescents seeing each movie and the amount of smoking contained in each one, the researchers estimated that these films delivered 13.9 billion smoking images. Sixty-one per cent of these were delivered by youth-rated movies.

The study in Germany, published today in the *American Journal of Preventive Medicine*, tested whether teens in a society where tobacco advertising is still rampant are as influenced by smoking on–screen. After controlling for demographic, media and psychosocial factors, investigators found that teens who had seen the most smoking in films (mostly US blockbusters) were more than twice as likely to have tried smoking than those who saw the least amount – results that mirror findings in the US.

The study in Mexico, as yet unpublished but presented at recent conferences, also found that, after controlling for all other factors known to influence whether teens start to smoke, exposure to on-screen smoking is strongly correlated with teens taking up cigarettes. So far, Germany and Mexico are the largest export markets for US films to replicate US cross-sectional studies of movie smoking and teen smoking.

These new reports come six weeks after the Harvard School of Public Health, invited by the Motion Picture Association of America (MPAA) to make recommendations on the tobacco question, advised the US film industry to 'eliminate the depiction of tobacco smoking from films accessible to children and youths'. The MPAA, which represents the major studios, has yet to respond publicly.

Tobacco control advocates around the globe are now calling on the film industry to curb smoking in films by:

⇨ requiring producers to certify in the credits that no person involved in the production of the film received payment for the use or display of tobacco

⇨ prohibiting the identification of tobacco brands in films

⇨ requiring strong anti-smoking ads to be shown prior to any film being shown that includes smoking scenes

⇨ giving future films containing tobacco images an 'adult' rating.

In addition, ASH urges actors to question the need to smoke in any film and to put pressure on producers to not include smoking unless it is editorially justified.

The US study found that just 30 actors delivered one-quarter of movie character smoking to young adolescents. These were primarily lead males who starred as smoking characters in multiple movies.

Deborah Arnott, Director of the health campaigning charity ASH, said:

'Popular actors can exert a huge influence on young, impressionable minds. Films are a major source of smoking imagery and teenagers are nearly three times as likely to try tobacco if they regularly watch actors smoke. If more actors refused to play smoking characters, fewer children would be exposed to smoking scenes and would be less likely to see smoking as a desirable activity.'

⇨ This information is reprinted with permission from ASH (Action on Smoking and Health). Visit www.ash.org.uk for more information.

Smoking regulations in England

Information from the UK Central Office of Information

On 1 July 2007, virtually all enclosed public places and workplaces in England became smokefree.

Places where you can't smoke

Under the new regulations, you are not permitted to smoke in:

⇨ pubs
⇨ bars
⇨ nightclubs
⇨ cafes
⇨ restaurants
⇨ membership clubs
⇨ shopping centres
⇨ public transport and work vehicles used by more than one person
⇨ indoor smoking rooms (for example at places of work).

Places where you can smoke

You are permitted to smoke in:

⇨ private dwellings
⇨ prisons
⇨ care homes
⇨ some pre-designated smoking rooms in hotels and guesthouses (although not dormitories)
⇨ Long-stay secure psychiatric facilities where patients stay for more than six months will be able to have smoking rooms until July 2008.

Exceptions

There are exceptions to the regulations. Your private dwelling does not have to be smokefree unless any parts of the dwelling are used solely for a place of work for:

⇨ more than one person who does not live in the dwelling
⇨ a person who lives at the dwelling and a person who does not
⇨ any person, whether they live at the dwelling or not, if people who don't live at the dwelling come to give or receive goods or services.

Penalties and fines

Breaking the smokefree law is a criminal offence. The fixed penalty notices and maximum fine for each offence are:

⇨ smoking in smokefree premises or work vehicles: a fixed penalty notice of £50 (reduced to £30 if paid in 15 days) for the person smoking, or a maximum fine of £200 if prosecuted and convicted by a court
⇨ failure to display no-smoking signs: a fixed penalty notice of £200 (reduced to £150 if paid in 15 days) for whoever manages or occupies the smokefree premises or vehicle – or a maximum fine of £1000 if prosecuted and convicted by a court

Local councils will be enforcing the new law in England.

If you see smoking in a smokefree area

You can call 0800 587 166 7 to report possible breaches of the law. This information will be passed to local councils to follow up, if appropriate.

⇨ This information is reprinted with permission from the UK Central Office of Information. Visit www.direct.gov.uk for more information.

© Crown copyright

Smoking ban 'to save 500,000 lives'

Information from the Press Association

At least half a million deaths a year are likely to be prevented by England's smoking ban, one of the world's leading experts on the deadly effects of tobacco has said.

Professor Sir Richard Peto made the forecast based on the experience of the Republic of Ireland, which introduced a similar ban in March 2004.

Irish cigarette sales have fallen by around 17% since the ban took effect. Sir Richard said if England followed a similar trend it could lead to around 1.5 million people quitting smoking. 'Half of all smokers are going to be killed by tobacco. If a million people stop smoking who wouldn't otherwise have done so then maybe you'll prevent half a million deaths,' he said.

The estimate of how many people might give up smoking as a result of the ban was a conservative one. He told a news conference in London: 'It's consistent with the idea that it does hit sales, and a lot of people are saying anecdotally that they want to use the ban to stop smoking.'

England's smoking ban will come into force at 6am on Sunday and will make the traditional smoke-filled pub a thing of the past. Under the ban it will be against the law to smoke in virtually all enclosed public places and workplaces, on public transport, and work vehicles used by more than one person and staff smoking rooms and indoor smoking areas will no longer be allowed.

Owners and managers of pubs, clubs and cafes face fines of up to £2,500 if they allow customers to smoke on their premises. Fixed penalties of £50, reduced to £30 if paid in 15 days, will be handed out to individuals caught smoking illegally.

Sir Richard, professor of medical statistics at Oxford University, has studied the population effects of smoking for 40 years. He worked closely with the late Professor Sir Richard Doll, who in the 1950s uncovered the first indisputable evidence that smoking causes lung cancer.

Since then, around seven million people in the UK and 100 million in other countries have died because of smoking, said Sir Richard. And despite the number of smokers halving from 20 to 10 million since 1950, about a quarter of deaths in middle age are still caused by smoking.

Sir Richard said preliminary unpublished results from a study of one million British women aged

> 'half of all smokers are going to be killed by tobacco. If a million people stop smoking who wouldn't otherwise have done so then maybe you'll prevent half a million deaths'

around 60 had highlighted the relationship between tobacco dose and death risk. Women who had smoked 20 cigarettes a day for most of their lives increased their risk of dying in middle age 30 times. Even smoking five cigarettes a day was associated with a six-fold increased risk of dying prematurely, and having just one cigarette doubled the risk.

The findings could have a bearing on the risks of passive smoking. The jury is still out on the extent to which inhaling other people's tobacco smoke is harmful to health. However, Sir Richard said there was no doubt it does cause some harm.

⇨ This article was published on 29 June 2007. It is reprinted with permission from the Press Association. Visit www.pressassociation.co.uk for more information.

© Press Association

Potential increase in pub patronage after ban

Information from Ipsos MORI

The advent of the smoking ban on 1st July is likely to bring an unexpected increase in custom to pubs and wine bars, according to new research conducted by Ipsos MORI.

Publicans should experience a significant increase in business, with 20% of regular or occasional drinkers in pubs/wine bars saying that they would visit pubs more regularly. This view was most strongly held amongst the nearly three-quarters of pub-goers who are non-smokers, amongst whom 26% said they would probably go to a pub more often. Among the total population, this translates to approximately 1.8 million adults in England and Wales (taking into account the difference between those who would go more often and less often).

Those visiting pubs and wine bars more often are most likely to be 35–44-year-olds, which may change the profile of these venues that currently tends to be more male and younger.

Younger adults (under 25 years of age) who are regular or occasional pub/wine bar-goers say that they will probably go less often (23%) after the smoking ban compared to 12% overall, reflecting heavier smoking amongst the under 35s (nearly one-third versus one quarter of population overall).

Regionally, the South is most likely to benefit from the smoking ban where there are currently more occasional drinkers.

Gill Aitchison, Head of Marketing Specialism, Ipsos MORI, comments:

'Our latest survey shows that the ban on smoking in enclosed public places is likely to boost business for publicans, who can expect to see 1.8 million more customers. It seems that amongst non-smokers, 13% would now visit a pub or wine bar more often, and this intention is surprisingly shared by 3% of smokers.'

'We anticipate that bars and pubs will become more popular because the majority of those questioned, some 72%, believe that the smoking ban would result in a more pleasant atmosphere. This opinion is so widespread that even 55% of smokers questioned agree with this statement. In order to fulfil customers' expectations, publicans will need to invest in their facilities, to appeal to broader age range and to women.'

⇨ This information is reprinted with permission from Ipsos MORI. Visit www.ipsos-mori.com for more information.

Attitudes of Londoners to the public smoking ban

The vast majority of Londoners (83%) support the Government's ban on smoking in public places according to an Ipsos MORI survey for the *Evening Standard*.

⇨ The research shows that most people (72%) strongly support such a ban — with only a small proportion of the public as a whole opposed to the ban (12%).

⇨ Even among smokers, a clear majority are in favour of the ban (64%).

⇨ The poll also shows that smokers are divided on whether the ban will lead to fewer people going to pubs or bars (45%) or whether it will not make any difference (45%).

⇨ Among non-smokers, there is a consensus that the ban will not make any difference (70%).

Notes:

⇨ *Results are based on telephone interviews with 1,003 residents in the Greater London area.*

⇨ *Interviews were conducted between 6–11 December 2006.*

⇨ *Data are weighted to reflect the London population profile.*

⇨ *Where results do not sum to 100%, this may be due to multiple responses, computer rounding or the exclusion of don't knows/not stated.*

Third of bosses to axe cigarette breaks

By Nick McDermott

More than a third of employers are planning to axe cigarette breaks when the smoking ban comes into force in England next month.

Lighting up in an enclosed public places will be illegal from 1 July, with those caught flouting the law facing a £50 on-the-spot fine or being summoned to court.

Premises that allow smoking — including 200,000 pubs and restaurants — will be fined up to £2,500.

It will bring an end to 'smoking rooms' in the workplace, with staff ordered outside if they want to have a cigarette break.

But many bosses will use the ban as an opportunity to end the practice, stopping their employees from taking time out during the working day to get their nicotine fix.

A survey of over 250 firms revealed that 36 per cent planned to axe smoking breaks when the ban becomes law.

But business leaders said such a move would be 'excessive', while trade union officials warned it could spark unrest and encourage staff to break the law.

TUC General Secretary Brendan Barber said: 'Lots of smokers see the ban as an opportunity to quit or cut down, but hardened nicotine addicts might not find giving up so easy. If employers decide to crack down on fag breaks, the danger is that some hardened smokers may try to find ways of flouting the ban.

'If going outside to smoke isn't an option, they may be tempted to smoke in secret on company premises.

'Employers should take a sensible approach to the ban and not use 1 July as a stick with which to beat their employees who smoke. Bosses should be thinking about ways of helping their staff stop smoking. Banning them from going outside for a quick

puff is not the answer.'

The ban, which will also apply to outdoor areas where bystanders are affected – such as bus shelters, football grounds, and train platforms – means staff must smoke in the open, outside their workplace.

A spokesman for the British Chambers of Commerce (BCC) said: 'There is a danger that the new smoking legislation could become more onerous than it needs to be. 'It is not illegal to smoke outside and, although non-smokers may find it annoying to see their colleagues nip out for a quick ciggie, it seems excessive to actually ban people from going to smoke.'

The report, by employment law advisors Consult GE, says there is little the nation's 12 million estimated smokers can do if their employers end cigarette breaks as they are not protected by law.

Stuart Chamberlain of Consult GEE said: 'Although there has never been a contractual right to smoke at work, companies seem keen to eradicate smoking among staff, and

the ban is giving them the impetus to do just that.

'Employees will struggle to fight any bans on their smoking breaks because they are not entitled to them.'

Smoking is the biggest cause of death and illness in the UK, with more than 120,000 people dying every year from smoking-related diseases. It is estimated one in five smokers will try and kick the habit once the ban is introduced next month.

Despite widespread backing, not everyone supports the smoking ban.

Antony Worrall Thompson, celebrity chef and patron of smokers' lobby group Forest, said: 'July 1 will be a sad day. Supporting smokers is worth doing. Nobody else wants to because they want to be politically correct.'

He has said previously: 'When you're an adult, life is about the freedom to choose. I think we're becoming more and more nannyish.'

Legal challenge to smoking ban

Information from the Press Association

Campaigners for the right to smoke are launching a High Court challenge over the Government's smoking ban in enclosed public places.

The ban, which starts on Sunday 1 July, covers virtually all enclosed public places including offices, factories, pubs and bars, but not outdoors or private homes.

The group says the ban amounts to injustice and erosion of freedom and personal liberties

The pressure group Freedom2Choose is planning to lodge papers at the Royal Courts of Justice in London seeking a judicial review.

The group says the ban amounts to injustice and erosion of freedom and personal liberties.

Their legal challenge is based on the contention that it violates human rights laws.

These include a breach of Article 1 of the First Protocol of the European Convention on Human Rights which guarantees the right to the peaceful enjoyment of possessions. Freedom2Choose also says the new laws are an 'unjustifiable' infringement of the right to respect for privacy under Article 8 of the convention.

The group says: 'This will be a legal test case with significant wider public interest.'

⇨ This information is reprinted with permission from the Press Association. Visit www.pressassociation.co.uk for more information.

© 2007 Press Association

'The group says the ban amounts to injustice and erosion of freedom and personal liberties.'

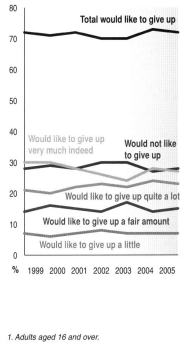

Giving up smoking

Main reasons for wanting to stop smoking, 2005, Great Britain

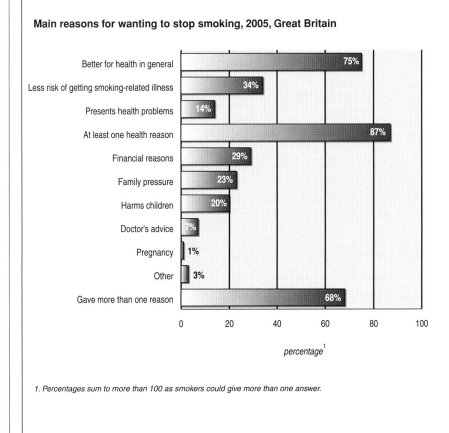

- Better for health in general — 75%
- Less risk of getting smoking-related illness — 34%
- Presents health problems — 14%
- At least one health reason — 87%
- Financial reasons — 29%
- Family pressure — 23%
- Harms children — 20%
- Doctor's advice — 7%
- Pregnancy — 1%
- Other — 3%
- Gave more than one reason — 68%

percentage[1]

1. Percentages sum to more than 100 as smokers could give more than one answer.

Views on giving up smoking[1], 1999-2005, Great Britain

- Total would like to give up
- Would like to give up very much indeed
- Would not like to give up
- Would like to give up quite a lot
- Would like to give up a fair amount
- Would like to give up a little

% 1999 2000 2001 2002 2003 2004 2005

1. Adults aged 16 and over.

Source: Smoking-Related Behaviour and Attitudes, 2005. Office for National Statistics. Crown copyright.

Smoking ban can seriously damage your brand

As smokers can no longer show off their 'status' packs of Marlboro or Camel in the pub, many are turning to cheaper ones, writes Mark Choueke

For anti-smoking campaigners, it may prove the ultimate victory: the last vestiges of glamour are being extinguished from an industry that has long prided itself on powerful brands and savvy marketing.

The imminent smoking ban in England and Wales is encouraging tobacco companies to chase each other downmarket with cut-price brands — even own-label varieties from shops such as Spar are being launched. If no one can see what you smoke in the pub, why bother paying a premium for an aspirational label?

It is a far cry from the days when Marlboro man ruled the roost. But smokers, a once loyal and resilient bunch, are switching to these brands rapidly to avoid being out of pocket as UK cigarette prices approach the £6 mark for a pack of 20.

The trend toward 'downtrading' has accelerated as marketers feel the impact of the advertising ban slapped on the tobacco industry in 2004. Few companies expect to launch high-end brands at all.

An industry executive admits: 'It is now much harder to launch a premium brand with no way to communicate the brand's strengths and no heritage to use as leverage. At least a budget brand can find a position in the market using its cut–price as the draw.'

Instead, all recent brand launches into the tobacco industry have come at the value end of the market where there is plenty of market growth and brand-building is minimal – Imperial Tobacco's Windsor Blue and Gallaher's Sterling brands are cases in point. Both have been leapt upon by consumers wishing to save their money. Price has replaced brand identity and smoothness of taste as the main driver of cigarette sales.

In the face of continuing long-term decline in the total number of cigarettes sold, 49 billion in 2006 compared to 51 billion in 2005, sales of cigarettes at the budget end of the market grew by three-quarters between 2001 and 2005 while sales in the premium category fell.

Those premium brands traditionally dominated the sector but now account for just 28 per cent of the market compared to value and economy brands which hold a 42 per cent market share.

Expensive brands will survive however and continue to make profit for retailers through innovation. Gallaher introduced 14-cigarette packs for its Benson & Hedges and Camel brands, believing the average smoker to get through 14 sticks a day. The company also recently introduced line extensions such as Silk Cut Graphite and the enticing sounding Camel Natural Flavour.

While one wonders what Camel smokers will make of this tacit admission that their cigarette brand has lacked in natural flavours all this time, it is clear the trading of new products under established names will continue, albeit under attack.

The ban on smoking in public places, which already exists in Ireland and Scotland and hits Wales within weeks and England in months, will continue to harm the cachet of the tobacco industry's top cigarette brands. Though cigarette makers admit that downtrading has happened and is ongoing, they insist that the trend has not eroded brand loyalty, which they say is still 'significant'. But anecdotal evidence from the Scottish experience and other cities such as New York where the smoking ban is already in action suggests while smoking may have gained in visibility due to more people smoking on the street, brands are less visible and perhaps, therefore, less important.

Smokers are said to be moving between pubs more frequently when they go out and having a drink in each place rather than staying in one bar all night. This way they can have a quick smoke en route to their next chosen venue. In a pleasing twist of irony, this will probably result in smokers getting more exercise than non-smokers on an average night out, but another outcome is cigarette packs won't be on show as much. Rather than your pack of Marlboro Lights, Lucky Strikes or Silk Cut sitting proudly on the pub table alongside your mobile phone, it will probably stay in your coat pocket most of the night.

If such 'badges', as branding expert Graham Hales refers to cigarette brands, aren't going to be on display, you might as well switch to Australian brand Winfield or Sky, Spar's own-label fag brand, both of which retail at under £4, rare bargains in today's market.

Hales, an executive director of branding consultancy Interbrand, says: 'Cigarette brands traditionally said a lot about you, as did your beer or jeans brand. Brands had distinct tastes and smokers trained themselves to enjoy a certain type. Smokers belonged loosely to clubs according to what pack they carried.

'That celebration of each brand has disappeared to be replaced by a general sense of shame as smokers increasingly incur the annoyance of society. And with so little that is positive about any cigarette brand and no way for brands to communicate what they represent, smokers are more likely than ever to shop around to get the best price. We've probably seen the last of premium cigarette brand launches.'

...WHAT PART OF A CAMEL DO THEY USE IN CIGARETTES?

...GOING ON THE SMELL...

Not surprisingly, an industry executive disagrees. 'Top brands will continue to sell, even if they are less visible – the brand you are attached to makes you feel good,' says the exec, 'otherwise why do people who are blatantly not on the pull still wear their good underwear when out on a Friday night? You don't need to show off your brand label to feel its power.'

Notwithstanding this splendid show of positivity, cigarette manufacturers must be worried about their future customers. Further legislation, set to come into effect in October, will see an increase in the age limit for purchasing tobacco from 16 to 18. With the number of new smokers in the future stemmed, and the habit of buying value brands already in evidence, how will cigarette companies entice future generations of smokers to buy their mainstream top brands?

Despite such stifling conditions, the UK tobacco industry is adept at looking after itself. Though numbers of cigarettes sold are on the wane, constant increases in the price of cigarettes means the value of sales has soared, hitting £12.6 billion last year. Cigarette companies place the blame for ever-spiralling cigarette prices on annual tax hikes. Alex

Parsons, head of media at Imperial Tobacco, which makes Lambert & Butler and Richmond, the UK's two leading FMCG brands, says:

'Between 77 per cent and 89 per cent of the price of cigarettes is made up of tax and that's why smokers have to make the tough decision to economise.'

Budget time has come round again and the tobacco industry is lobbying Gordon Brown to freeze taxes on cigarettes. The Tobacco Manufacturers' Association warns that criminals are taking advantage of the fact that UK cigarettes are the most expensive in Europe. Figures show a growing industry of opportunists buying cigarettes abroad on the cheap and smuggling them across the border. Others counterfeit cigarettes altogether so the product does not match the brand marked on the packaging.

While the £18 billion worth of non-duty-paid cigarettes Brits bought last year included those bought legally through cross-border shopping, it is estimated by customs that two thirds of those cigarettes were in the UK illegally. An industry source says: 'Smuggled or counterfeit cigarettes are sadly growing in abundance.

'celebration of each brand has disappeared to be replaced by a general sense of shame as smokers increasingly incur the annoyance of society'

'They're the ones you find at car boot sales or sold by street vendors or irresponsible retailers for a fraction of the recommended retail price. An increase in tax on tobacco above the line of inflation would be an encouragement of illegal activity.'

The pressure is on the Government though to raise taxes on cigarettes as anti-smoking campaigners continue to publicise the dangers of smoking — in 2005 the Department of Health invested more than £14 million in anti-smoking campaigns.

In case anyone was beginning to take pity on the tobacco industry, however, for being stuck in an industry where the prices of its products are beyond its control and in the hands of politicians, market research company Mintel International notes that while rising tax has been a factor in cigarette cost increases, 'price rises by manufacturers have far exceeded the extra duty that has been added'.

Whatever the reason behind the cost of cigarettes, the effect on the smoker is plain. Ellen Watson, a 27-year-old smoker of 11 years from Croydon, used to smoke Benson & Hedges, but says rolling her own cigarettes now saves her some £125 per month. Watson admits she lives with traditional stigmas attached to roll-your-own tobacco brands. 'Tobacco pouches are a bit "old man" and I think people at work see you rolling cigarettes and assume you spend your weekend just smoking spliffs. But it's quite a prominent habit among people my age now because cigarettes are simply too expensive.'

⇨ This article first appeared in the Telegraph on 12 March 2007.
© 2007 Telegraph Group Limited

Hundreds complain about anti-smoking ads

Information from National News

A hard-hitting anti-smoking campaign showing smokers being dragged by fish hooks through their cheeks has been partially banned after triggering hundreds of complaints.

The Department of Health ads shown on TV, posters and in newspapers, which depicted men and women being pulled along by hooks attached to their faces to warn smokers of the difficulties of quitting, attracted more than 700 complaints.

One TV ad showed a women being hauled along the floor through her house by the hook, followed by a man in the street being hauled along the ground, over a car bonnet and into a corner shop.

The ads stated 'If you're a smoker, getting unhooked isn't easy', and urged smokers to 'Get unhooked', directing them to NHS helplines on the internet and telephone.

Other ads appeared in newspapers, showing men and women with pained expressions with a taught wire pulling on a hook attached to their lips. Further ads were posted on-line.

The campaign attracted hundreds of complaints, with parents saying that the adverts had upset or frightened their children and that they were 'offensive, frightening or distressing'.

More than 150 parents said that the posters had scared their kids, aged between two and 15, while 103 complained that the TV ads had frightened their youngsters, aged between two and 12.

The TV ads were cleared by the Broadcast Advertising Clearance Centre but with an ex-kids restriction, meaning they could not be shown in or around programmes targeted at children.

Fewer but similar complaints were

raised about the newspaper ads and a lower number still raised objections about the internet campaign.

The Department of Health conceded that some people may find the violent nature of the ads disturbing but said they did not believe viewers would be seriously offended given the nature of the anti-smoking message.

Despite the level of complaint, they argued that hard-hitting campaigns would always generate objections, pointing out they had received praise over the ads from medical experts and members of the public.

They said that the ads were not meant to be gratuitous and pointed out smoking was the UK's greatest cause of preventable illness and death. Any fear created by the ads would 'pale into insignificance' compared to the harmed caused by smoking, said the DoH.

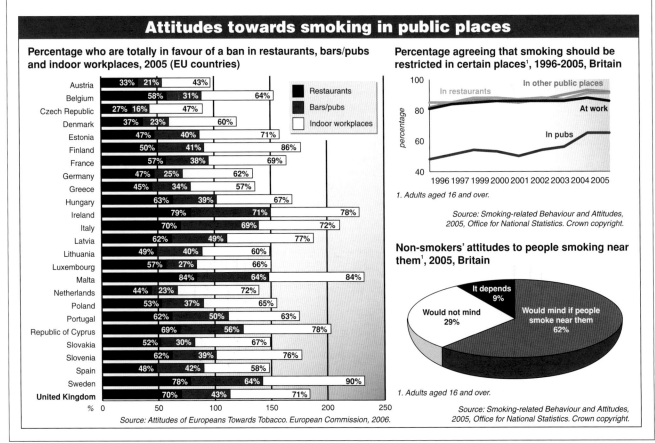

Attitudes towards smoking in public places

Percentage who are totally in favour of a ban in restaurants, bars/pubs and indoor workplaces, 2005 (EU countries)

Source: Attitudes of Europeans Towards Tobacco. European Commission, 2006.

Percentage agreeing that smoking should be restricted in certain places[1], 1996-2005, Britain

1. Adults aged 16 and over.

Source: Smoking-related Behaviour and Attitudes, 2005, Office for National Statistics. Crown copyright.

Non-smokers' attitudes to people smoking near them[1], 2005, Britain

It depends 9%
Would not mind 29%
Would mind if people smoke near them 62%

1. Adults aged 16 and over.

Source: Smoking-related Behaviour and Attitudes, 2005, Office for National Statistics. Crown copyright.

The posters were deliberately not placed near schools and the DoH argued that the ads had avoided focusing on smoking-related illnesses, perceived by smokers as problems for the future, and instead concentrated on the addictive nature of cigarettes.

Since the launch of the campaign, 83,606 smokers phoned the NHS Smoking Helpline, 545,564 had visited the gosmokefree website, 195,000 had had interactions with the TV pages and 6,743 had made contact via SMS.

The BACC said they had been aware of the TV ads' potential to distress viewers, particularly younger viewers, when they cleared them.

But they argued the public were more prepared to accept provocative images in ads if they were for an organisation promoting health and safety rather than a commercial advertiser.

Making its ruling, the ASA upheld the complaints against certain of the ads but acknowledged the message of the dangers of smoking was in the public interest.

It ruled that the poster campaign should not be repeated and that the ex-kids restriction was insufficient for the TV ads.

An ASA spokesman said: 'We considered that, although the posters' images were shocking, they had the worthwhile purpose of discouraging smoking. We considered that, because adults were likely to understand the seriousness of the anti-smoking message, the posters' images were

unlikely to cause them serious offence or distress.

'We noted, however, the posters showed the hooks clearly piercing the cheeks of the addicted smokers who, we considered, looked distressed and in pain.

'We noted that, although the posters had not been placed near schools, they had appeared in places where they could easily be seen by children.

'We considered that, although the posters highlighted the perils of tobacco addiction and discouraged smoking, because they were untargeted, and realistically and graphically showed the piercing of the cheek with a hook, they were likely to frighten and distress children.

'We noted that, although the TV ads had been given an ex-kids

restriction, which was likely to prevent most very young children from seeing them, they would still be shown at times when they could be seen by older children.

'We noted 103 complainants had referred to children aged between three and 12 years old who had been frightened and distressed by the TV ads.'

However, complaints about the newspaper, magazine and internet ads were not upheld.

The ASA said: 'We told DoH not to repeat the posters and told them that the TV ads' ex-kids restriction was insufficient.'

⇨ This article appeared on the Life Style Extra website on 16 May 2007. Visit www.lse.co.uk for more information.

© National News

Ten-pack ban may cut teen smoking

By Rosie Murray-West

The days of teenagers fuelling their smoking habits by buying cigarettes in cheaper packs of 10 could be numbered, under radical proposals being considered by the Department of Health.

Leading doctors have drawn up recommendations to reduce the number of young people smoking, including banning the smaller packs of cigarettes and keeping tobacco out of sight in shops.

The proposals, contained in a report from the British Medical Association (BMA), also include plans to ban tobacco-vending machines and impose regular price increases to try to cut demand.

The BMA report says 55 per cent of teenagers who smoke last bought cigarettes in a pack of 10. Although under-age smoking rates have fallen in England, a fifth of teenagers are regular smokers.

⇨ This article first appeared in the Telegraph on the 24th of April, 2007.

© 2007 Telegraph Group Limited

Young people and nicotine patches

Interviews by Gavin Mather

Smokers as young as twelve are to be offered nicotine patches to help them quit – young people aren't all sure that's the best solution.

Claire Hughes, 12, Blakelaw

I don't think children should smoke because you can get cancer. And I don't think nicotine patches should be given to children either. None of my friends smoke. When I'm older, if I have children that smoke, I would ground them.

Amy Soanes, 9, Cowgate

Children shouldn't smoke because it's bad for them. I think nicotine patches for children is a good idea because it will stop them smoking. I think smoking should be made illegal for everyone because it's destroying people's health. I think stress makes young people smoke. I don't have any friends who smoke. There's nothing good about smoking.

Sarah Gurkin, 11, Blakelaw

Smoking gives you cancer when you're older. I don't think children having nicotine patches is a good idea. I think smoking should be banned because it's bad for you. I think young people get into smoking through people daring them and things like that.

Ashley Warneford, 14, Lobley Hill

It's not a good idea for children to smoke because it can damage their health. I think patches for children is a good thing because it will stop them from smoking and help them. I think smoking should be made illegal because people are dying from it. I think young people start to smoke because their friends do it.

Stephanie Wilson, 11, Blakelaw

Young people shouldn't smoke because they can damage themselves and when they get older they might regret it. You can also damage others if you smoke around them. I don't agree with nicotine patches for children. If a child has done something wrong, you would tell them not to do it again, and they would have to learn how to control it.

I think children start smoking because they see adults do it and they copy. If I ever had children who smoked I would explain how it can damage them and if they didn't take notice I would stop them from going out.

Samantha Newby, 13, Cowgate

Children shouldn't smoke because it's bad for their health and it costs too much money. I don't think it's a good idea for kids to have nicotine patches to stop them smoking. It's their own fault for smoking anyway. I don't think it's a good idea to ban smoking for everyone, because some parents might be under a lot of stress.

I think young people start to smoke because they want to be like their friends. They also get it from their parents I think. Some people smoke because they know they're doing something wrong and they like the danger of it. Practically all of my friends smoke.

Kayleigh Warneford, 12, Lobley Hill

Children shouldn't smoke. I don't really think nicotine patches are a

good idea for children to help them stop though. I think smoking should not be allowed at all for anyone. If my mam smoked and something happened to her I wouldn't be happy. I think children smoke to look good.

Andrea Dixon, 15, Blakelaw

I don't think children should smoke. If you smoke, you die. I think nicotine patches are a good idea, especially during your teenage years when you might get addicted. They should be given a try. To my mind it doesn't make any difference if we make smoking legal or not, people are still going to do it. I think peer pressure makes people start smoking.

⇨ This article was published in the *Newcastle Evening Chronicle* in 2001.

National smoking map shows poverty link

Information from Cancer Research UK

A map showing the number of smokers across the UK provides a graphic insight into the links between smoking and poverty, say campaigners.

Smoking remains the single biggest factor behind the difference in life expectancy between social classes in the UK, said researchers Action on Smoking and Health (ASH).

The map was produced by combining government data on smoking rates and poverty, providing a graphic illustration of the underlying factors which link the two.

Just 20 per cent of men and 17 per cent of women in professional and managerial jobs are likely to smoke,

CANCER RESEARCH UK

compared to 34 per cent of men and 30 per cent of women in manual and routine work.

Earlier research has shown that 48 per cent of men in the poorest groups die before they reach 70, compared to 22 per cent of men in the richest classes.

Around half of this difference was said to be due to tobacco use. ASH has called for councils across the UK to use the data to inform anti-tobacco programmes.

'Smoking is the biggest killer in England, and it kills more people in poorer communities than in richer ones,' said director of ASH Deborah Arnott.

'We hope that local councils, NHS primary care trusts, MPs and decision makers will use these maps as part of their work on tobacco control.

'This project shows once again why smoking must be top of the list of concerns for everyone who cares about tackling poverty and social exclusion.'

⇨ This information is reprinted with permission from Cancer Research UK. Visit www.cancerresearchuk.org for more information.

© Cancer Research UK

The prevalence of smoking

Prevalence of smoking among European Union countries, by smoking status, 2004

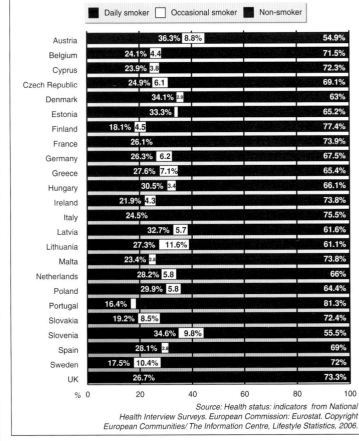

Legend: ■ Daily smoker □ Occasional smoker ■ Non-smoker

Country	Daily smoker	Occasional smoker	Non-smoker
Austria	36.3%	8.8%	54.9%
Belgium	24.1%	4.4	71.5%
Cyprus	23.9%	3.8	72.3%
Czech Republic	24.9%	6.1	69.1%
Denmark	34.1%	2.9	63%
Estonia	33.3%		65.2%
Finland	18.1%	4.5	77.4%
France	26.1%		73.9%
Germany	26.3%	6.2	67.5%
Greece	27.6%	7.1%	65.4%
Hungary	30.5%	3.4	66.1%
Ireland	21.9%	4.3	73.8%
Italy	24.5%		75.5%
Latvia	32.7%	5.7	61.6%
Lithuania	27.3%	11.6%	61.1%
Malta	23.4%	2.8	73.8%
Netherlands	28.2%	5.8	66%
Poland	29.9%	5.8	64.4%
Portugal	16.4%		81.3%
Slovakia	19.2%	8.5%	72.4%
Slovenia	34.6%	9.8%	55.5%
Spain	28.1%	2.8	69%
Sweden	17.5%	10.4%	72%
UK	26.7%		73.3%

Source: Health status: indicators from National Health Interview Surveys. European Commission: Eurostat. Copyright European Communities/ The Information Centre, Lifestyle Statistics, 2006.

Prevalence of cigarette smoking among adults, by gender and Government Office Region, 2004, England

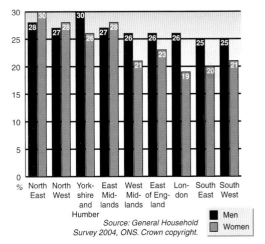

Regions: North East, North West, Yorkshire and Humber, East Midlands, West Midlands, East of England, London, South East, South West

Legend: ■ Men ■ Women

Source: General Household Survey 2004, ONS. Crown copyright.

Prevalence of cigarette smoking among adults, by age and gender, 1948, and 1980 to 2000

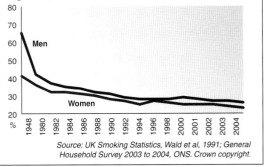

Source: UK Smoking Statistics, Wald et al, 1991; General Household Survey 2003 to 2004, ONS. Crown copyright.

Tobacco in the developing world

Information from ASH

The World Health Organisation (WHO) estimates that approximately 5 million people die each year worldwide from tobacco-related illnesses. If current trends continue, this figure will rise to about 10 million per year by 2025.

Prevalence and consumption

Tobacco consumption has fallen over the past 20 years in most high-income countries such as Britain, Canada, the United States, Australia and most northern European countries. Demand is projected to continue to fall, dropping to 2.05 million tonnes in 2010. This is 10 per cent lower than the 1998 figure. By contrast, tobacco consumption rates in the developing countries are expected to increase to 5.09 million tonnes – a 1.7 per cent growth rate between 1998 and 2010. About 80 percent of this increase in demand is expected to be in the Far East, particularly China.

Worldwide, approximately 1.3 billion people smoke cigarettes or other tobacco products: almost one billion men and 250 million women. Globally, tobacco use is significantly higher amongst men (47%) than it is amongst women (12%). In most developing nations this is partly due to cultural traditions, although the situation is changing and more women are taking up smoking in response to the marketing tactics of the tobacco industry. In developed countries 35% of men and 22% of women smoke, while in developing countries 50% of men and 9% of women are smokers. Women in developing countries are clearly a key potential market for the tobacco industry. Recent increases in female smoking prevalence have been reported from Cambodia, Malaysia and Bangladesh.

The spread of smoking to the developing world

The large multinational tobacco companies based in Britain and the USA are largely responsible for the spread of the smoking habit to developing countries. The entry of a multinational tobacco company into a new market is typically accompanied by sophisticated and effective advertising and promotional activities, often leading national tobacco companies to step up their marketing activities in response. As a result, overall expenditure on advertising increases with a corresponding rise in tobacco consumption and huge impact on human health.

In July 2004, British American Tobacco (BAT) announced plans to manufacture cigarettes in China, although this is subject to confirmation by the Chinese authorities. If it goes ahead, the deal with local partner, China Eastern Investments, will involve building an £800million factory with a capacity of 100bn a year.

Figures for 1998 reveal that 4% of Chinese women smoke, up from 3% in 1991. For BAT, persuading more Chinese women to smoke is a huge marketing opportunity. Even as long ago as 1915 BAT had business interests in China and was instrumental in encouraging the Chinese people to smoke. Within 30 years, China's annual consumption of cigarettes rose from a negligible number to 100 billion 9 and by 1994 it stood at 1,646 billion.

Following World War II, the USA began exporting tobacco under the 'Food for Peace' programme. In the first 25 years of the programme, the US exported almost $1 billion worth of tobacco. This project exposed developing countries to Western-style cigarettes. By the late 1960s, the leading US and UK companies were selling to dozens of countries. During the 1980s, international sales rose dramatically. In 1994, 220 billion US-manufactured cigarettes were shipped abroad, a 55% increase since 1989. In the year 2000 the US exported 148,261 million cigarettes.

Asian countries in particular have been the target of US tobacco companies. During the 1980s, the US Government threatened trade sanctions against Japan, Taiwan, South Korea and Thailand unless they opened up their markets to American cigarettes. All four countries gave in to US pressure but Thailand later won the right to ban cigarette advertising under a ruling by the General Agreement on Tariffs and Trade (GATT) which ruled that countries could give 'priority to human health over trade liberalisation'. Since the lifting of import restrictions, the Asian countries have witnessed a dramatic increase in smoking: South Korea's cigarette consumption rose from 68,000 tonnes in 1980–82 to 101,000 tonnes in 1999, whilst consumption in Thailand over the same period grew from 31,000 tonnes to 40,000 tonnes.

Economic impact

Although tobacco is grown in more than 100 countries, just five countries – China, USA, India, Brazil and Turkey – account for almost two-thirds of global production. Only two countries – Malawi and Zimbabwe – are significantly dependent on export earnings from tobacco. In 2002, Japan Tobacco, Philip Morris/Altria and BAT, the world's three largest tobacco multinationals, had combined tobacco revenues of more than US$ 121 billion. This sum was greater than the total combined GDP of 27 developing countries.

Faced with the offer of jobs, revenue, exports and foreign exchange, governments of developing countries find it difficult to resist especially when 'aid' is also offered.

Although the initial cost of seed, tools, curing barns, etc. is high, the multinational tobacco companies make loans to small farmers for fertiliser and insecticides, thus trapping them into a cycle of debt. It has also been claimed that several large tobacco companies collude and exercise overweening influence on tobacco growers. They decide prices amongst themselves and severely punish growers who decide to sell their crop elsewhere. Growers are effectively squeezed, with many farmers driven deeper in debt to the tobacco companies.

In the past, tobacco has been supported as a cash crop by the FAO (United Nations Food and Agriculture Organisation), the World Bank and other governmental agencies. However, in 1992 the World Bank stopped giving loans for growing tobacco. A cost–benefit analysis of tobacco growing for developing countries has shown that the short-term gains are likely to be offset by long-term costs.

Multinational tobacco companies often seek to strengthen their presence in developing countries by engaging in their economies and communities. Seemingly philanthropic acts of building schools and hospitals have allowed the tobacco companies to buy into health and education sectors of society. Poorer developing nations are less likely to resist such financial aid and look favourably on the tobacco industry.

Health effects

In industrialised countries, smoking has been identified as the most important preventable cause of disease and premature death. Cigarettes kill half of all lifetime users and tobacco kills more than AIDS, legal drugs, illegal drugs, road accidents, murder and suicide combined. By 2030, a projected 7 million people in developing countries will be killed every year by tobacco. China alone (with 20% of the world's population) suffers almost a million deaths a year from tobacco, a figure that is likely to at least double by 2025. A study in Bangladesh has shown that tobacco consumption has a direct impact on the health of poor households, with poorer people spending less on food, resulting in malnutrition. The study found that the typical poor smoker could add over 500 calories to the diet of one or two children with his or her daily tobacco expenditure. Applied to the whole country, an estimated 10.5 million people currently malnourished could have an adequate diet if money spent on tobacco were spent on food instead. A packet of Marlboro cigarettes, or equivalent brand, will buy a dozen eggs in Panama, a kilogram of fish in Ghana or six kilograms of rice in Bangladesh.

The effects of tobacco use may be worsened by the incidence of infectious disease and environmental hazards in the developing world that may cause increases in certain cancers. Occupational hazards such as organic dusts, uranium or asbestos can act as synergistic carcinogens in workers.

Environmental impact

Almost three-quarters of the world's tobacco is grown in developing countries. Serious environmental costs are associated with tobacco production, especially deforestation, erosion and desertification. There is also an increased risk of fires resulting from cigarette smoking in countries where dwellings are often constructed of highly flammable materials. (For more information on the environmental impact of tobacco see ASH Fact Sheet no. 22, *Tobacco & the Environment*.)

Tobacco control

As the tobacco industry is able to wield so much power over the governments of the poorer countries, regulations to control smoking tend to be weak. Advertising restrictions are few, or negligible, and tar levels of cigarettes sold in developing countries tend to be significantly higher than in brands sold in the USA or Europe. Advertising tends to reflect the aspirations of the poor to emulate the West. For example in Africa, brand names include 'Diplomat' (Ghana), 'High Society' (Nigeria), 'Sportsman' and 'Champion' (both Kenya). More than 40 developing countries do not require health warnings to appear on cigarette packs, and of those that do, 73% require weakly worded warnings, often in English rather than in local languages. There are some commendable exceptions: South Africa, Thailand and Singapore all have comprehensive tobacco control laws including bans on tobacco advertising and sponsorship, smoke-free public places, large clear health warnings, and health education campaigns.

⇨   This information is reprinted with permission from ASH (Action on Smoking and Health). Visit www.ash.org.uk for more information.

© ASH 2007

Smoking in developing countries

Information from Cancer Research UK

There are around 1,100 million regular smokers in the world today, of which approximately 300 million are in economically developed countries and 800 million in the developing world.

While lung cancer deaths in the UK and other developed countries are now in decline, they are increasing very rapidly in many developing countries where smoking prevalence is high and general awareness of the risks of smoking is relatively low.

Developing countries offer an attractive marketing opportunity for tobacco manufacturers, whose Western markets are shrinking. Tobacco companies have been able to promote tobacco use in these countries, often with the help and support of their own governments via trade agreements.

Our research

Professors Richard Peto and Rory Colins in Oxford are monitoring the epidemic of death from tobacco in several countries including China. They have shown that worldwide deaths from tobacco are likely to increase from about 4 million per year at present to about 10 million per year by the time children of today reach middle age. Around 70 per cent of these deaths will be in developing countries.

Recommended measures

A range of measures need to be adopted to curb the growing tobacco epidemic in developing countries. Strategies, which have proved successful in the West over several decades, could be adopted by developing countries to prevent further growth in tobacco use. Effective public health and information programmes should be combined with significant taxation and with bans on all forms of tobacco advertising and promotion.

Cancer Research UK believes that the concept of wealthy countries,

CANCER RESEARCH UK

like the UK or USA, exporting the burden of death and disease to poorer countries, via tobacco promotion, is abhorrent. Tobacco control is now a global problem.

Treaty on tobacco control

In recognition of this the 192 Member States of the World Health Organisation set up an international treaty on tobacco control (Framework Convention on Tobacco Control – FCTC). The world's first public health treaty, the FCTC contains a host of measures designed to reduce the devastating health and economic impacts of tobacco. The final agreement, reached in May 2003 after nearly four years of negotiations, provides the basic tools for countries to enact comprehensive tobacco control legislation. Provisions in the treaty encourage countries to:
⇨ Enact comprehensive bans on tobacco advertising, promotion and sponsorship; Place rotating health warnings on tobacco packaging that cover at least 30

per cent (but ideally 50 per cent or more) of the principal display areas and can include pictures.
⇨ Ban the use of misleading and deceptive terms such as 'light' and 'mild'; Protect citizens from exposure to tobacco smoke in workplaces, public transport and indoor public places.
⇨ Combat smuggling, including the placing of final destination markings on packs.
⇨ Increase tobacco taxes.

The FCTC also contains numerous other measures designed to promote and protect public health, such as mandating the disclosure of ingredients in tobacco products, providing treatment for tobacco addiction, encouraging legal action against the tobacco industry, and promoting research and the exchange of information among countries.

The FCTC was adopted unanimously by the World Health Assembly on 21 May 2003 and was closed for signature on 29 June 2004.

Currently, 148 countries, including the UK, have ratified this treaty, meaning that it is legally binding. A subsidiary body, the Conference of the Parties, has met twice since the treaty entered into force in 2005, and progress has been made in a number of key areas.

The Framework Convention is only legally binding on countries that ratify it. The onus will be on national governments to implement the FCTC and protocols. How effective the FCTC will be in reversing the tobacco epidemic will be determined by the fully governments implement the obligations contained in the FCTC.

⇨ This information is reprinted with permission from Cancer Research UK. Visit www.cancerresearchuk.org for more information.

© Cancer Research UK

How nicotine works

By Ann Meeker-O'Connell

For thousands of years, people have smoked or chewed the leaves of the tobacco plant, *Nicotiana tabacum*. Tobacco was first found and cultivated in the Americas, perhaps as early as 6000 BC. Following the discovery and colonisation of North and South America, the tobacco plant was exported widely, to continental Europe and the rest of the civilised world. Even in its early days, tobacco use was controversial. Some hailed its medicinal properties. For example, tobacco was supposed to be protective against the ravages of the Plague! As early as the 1600s, people speculated that there might be a link between diseases, like cancer, and tobacco use. Since then, modern research methods have provided evidence of this link, and public service announcements that warn of tobacco's health risks and addictive nature are seen regularly on TV.

What is it about tobacco that makes people so compelled to use it despite all of the admonitions? Smoking or chewing tobacco makes people feel good, even mildly euphoric. While there are thousands of chemicals in the tobacco plant (not to mention those added by cigarette manufacturers), one, nicotine, produces all the good feelings that draw people back for another cigarette or plug of tobacco. In this article, we'll examine nicotine and how it affects the human body.

What is nicotine?

Nicotine ($C_{10}H_{14}N_2$) is a naturally occurring liquid alkaloid. An alkaloid is an organic compound made out of carbon, hydrogen, nitrogen and sometimes oxygen. These chemicals have potent effects on the human body. For example, many people regularly enjoy the stimulating effects of another alkaloid, caffeine, as they quaff a cup or two of coffee in the morning.

Nicotine normally makes up about 5% of a tobacco plant, by weight. Cigarettes contain 8–20 milligrams (mg) of nicotine (depending on the brand), but only approximately 1mg is actually absorbed by your body when you smoke a cigarette.

Nicotine in the body

As with most addictive substances, humans have devised a number of ways of delivering nicotine to their bodies. Nicotine readily diffuses through:
⇨ Skin
⇨ Lungs
⇨ Mucous membranes (such as the lining of your nose or your gums).

Nicotine moves right into the small blood vessels that line the tissues listed above. From there, nicotine travels through your bloodstream to the brain, and then is delivered to the rest of your body.

The most common (and the most expedient way) to get nicotine and other drugs into your bloodstream is through inhalation – by smoking it. Your lungs are lined by millions of alveoli, the tiny air sacs where gas exchange occurs. These alveoli provide an enormous surface area – 90 times greater than that of your skin – and thus provide ample access for nicotine and other compounds. Once in your bloodstream, nicotine flows almost immediately to your brain. Although nicotine takes a lot of different actions throughout your body, what it does in the brain is responsible for both the good feelings you get from smoking, as well as the irritability you feel if you try to quit. Within 10 to 15 seconds of inhaling, most smokers are in the throes of nicotine's effects.

Nicotine doesn't stick around your body for too long. It has a half-life of about 60 minutes, meaning that six hours after a cigarette, only about 0.031mg of the 1mg of nicotine you inhaled remains in your body.

How does your body get rid of nicotine?

Here's the process:

⇨ About 80 per cent of nicotine is broken down to cotinine by enzymes in your liver.

⇨ Nicotine is also metabolised in your lungs to cotinine and nicotine oxide.

⇨ Cotinine and other metabolites are excreted in your urine. Cotinine has a 24-hour half-life, so you can test whether or not someone has been smoking in the past day or two by screening his or her urine for cotinine.

⇨ The remaining nicotine is filtered from the blood by your kidneys and excreted in the urine.

Different people metabolise nicotine at different rates. Some people even have a genetic defect in the enzymes in their liver that break down nicotine, whereby the mutant enzyme is much less effective at metabolising nicotine than the normal variant. If a person has this gene, their blood and brain nicotine levels stay higher for longer after smoking a cigarette. Normally, people keep smoking cigarettes throughout the day to maintain a steady level of nicotine in their bodies. Smokers with this gene usually end up smoking many fewer cigarettes, because they don't constantly need more nicotine.

Effects of nicotine

Nicotine changes how your brain and your body function. The net results are somewhat of a paradox: nicotine can both invigorate and relax a smoker, depending on how much and how often they smoke. This biphasic effect is not uncommon. Although the actions of nicotine and ethanol in the body are quite different, you also see dose-dependent effects when you drink alcoholic beverages. Your first drink may loosen your inhibitions and fire you up, but after several drinks, you're usually pretty sedate.

Nicotine and the body

Nicotine initially causes a rapid release of adrenaline, the 'fight-or-flight' hormone. If you've ever jumped in fright at a scary movie or rushed around the office trying to finish a project by your deadline, you may be familiar with adrenaline's effects:

⇨ Rapid heartbeat
⇨ Increased blood pressure
⇨ Rapid, shallow breathing.

Adrenaline also tells your body to dump some of its glucose stores into your blood. This makes sense if you remind yourself that the 'fight-or-flight' response is meant to help you either defend yourself from a hungry predator or hightail it out of a dangerous situation – running or brawling both require plenty of energy to fuel your muscles.

Nicotine itself may also block the release of the hormone insulin. Insulin tells your cells to take up excess glucose from your blood. This means that nicotine makes people somewhat hyperglycemic, having more sugar than usual in their blood. Some people think that nicotine also curbs their appetite so that they eat less. This hyperglycemia could be one explanation why: their bodies and brain may see the excess sugar and down-regulate the hormones and other signals that are perceived as hunger.

Nicotine may also increase your basal metabolic rate slightly. This means that you burn more calories than you usually would when you are just sitting around. However, losing weight by smoking doesn't give you any of the health benefits that you'd get if you were losing weight by exercising – it actually does the opposite! Over the long haul, nicotine can increase the level of the 'bad' cholesterol, LDL, that damages your arteries. This makes it more likely that you could have a heart attack or a stroke.

Addiction

Billions of dollars have been spent in the United States fighting over whether or not nicotine is addictive. The position of the medical and scientific communities is that nicotine is most definitely

addictive. Nicotine meets both the psychological and physiological measures of addiction:

Psychological

People who are addicted to something will use it compulsively, without regard for its negative effects on their health or their life. A good example would be someone who continues to smoke, even as they use an oxygen tank to breathe because of the damage smoking has done to their lungs.

Physiological

Neuroscientists call anything that turns on the reward pathway in the brain addictive. Because stimulating this neural circuitry makes you feel so good, you may continue to do it again and again to get those feelings back.

Nicotine's effects are short-lived, lasting only 40 minutes to a couple of hours. This leads people to smoke or chew tobacco periodically throughout the day to dose themselves with nicotine. Add to this the fact that you can become tolerant to nicotine's effects – you need to use more and more nicotine to reach the same degree of stimulation or relaxation – and you can see how people would quickly move from smoking one cigarette to a pack-a-day habit.

Withdrawal

What happens when smokers abruptly stop using nicotine? While you're using nicotine-containing products, your body adapts the way it works to compensate for the effects of the nicotine. For example, neurons in your brain might increase or decrease the number of receptors or the amount of different neurotransmitters affected by the presence of nicotine. When you no longer have nicotine in your body, these physiological adaptations for nicotine remain. The net result is that your body can't function the same way in the absence of the drug as it did before, at least in the short term. People trying to quit nicotine experience this as:

⇨ irritability
⇨ anxiety
⇨ depression

⇨ craving for nicotine.

Over a period of about a month, these symptoms and the physiological changes subside. But for many smokers, even a day without nicotine is excruciating. Every year, millions of people try to break the nicotine habit; only 10 percent of them succeed. Most people throw in the towel after less than a week of trying, because the way that nicotine rewires the reward system in the brain makes nicotine's pull irresistible.

Toxicity

Anti-smoking advocates highlight the long-term health effects, like cancer and emphysema, that result from a lifetime of smoking or chewing tobacco – but these maladies are the result of chemicals in cigarettes other than nicotine. Unfortunately, the fact that nicotine alone is an extremely toxic poison often goes unmentioned. Not many people realise that nicotine is also sold commercially in the form of a pesticide! And every year, many children go to the emergency room after eating cigarettes or cigarette butts. Sixty milligrams of nicotine (about the amount in three or four cigarettes if all of the nicotine were absorbed) will kill an adult, but consuming only one cigarette's worth of nicotine is enough to make a toddler severely ill!

⇨ This information is reprinted with permission from HowStuffWorks. Visit www.howstuffworks.com for more information.

Benefits timeline

What happens when you quit smoking

From as little as 20 minutes after your last cigarette, your body will begin to reap the benefits of stopping smoking. Don't forget that, with continued abstinence, your health will continue to profit from not smoking through prolonged life and reduced risk of smoking-related illness.

It is never too late to stop smoking and, no matter how young or old you are, you will experience a healthier and better quality of life once you quit. This timeline gives you an overview of some of the benefits you can look forward to:

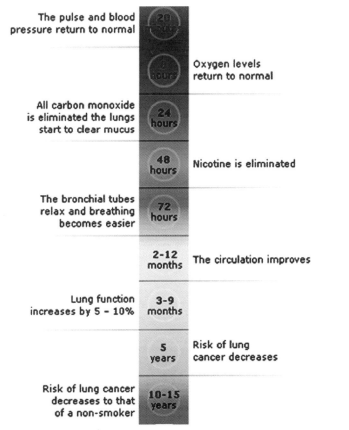

The pulse and blood pressure return to normal — 20 hours

Oxygen levels return to normal — 8 hours

All carbon monoxide is eliminated the lungs start to clear mucus — 24 hours

Nicotine is eliminated — 48 hours

The bronchial tubes relax and breathing becomes easier — 72 hours

The circulation improves — 2-12 months

Lung function increases by 5 – 10% — 3-9 months

Risk of lung cancer decreases — 5 years

Risk of lung cancer decreases to that of a non-smoker — 10-15 years

⇨ This information is reprinted with permission from the NHS Quit Smoking Service for Enfield and Haringey. Visit www.quitsmoking.uk.com for more information.

Smoking less 'is no healthier'

By Nicole Martin

Smokers who cut down rather than quit in the hope of improving their health might be wasting their time, researchers said yesterday. They reviewed a series of studies and found there was no evidence that smoking fewer cigarettes reduced the risk of developing potentially fatal diseases.

Lindsay Stead, the lead researcher from the Department of Primary Care at Oxford University, said that people who cut down tended to smoke harder, deeper and longer than before to get the nicotine fix they needed.

'Cutting down is not a satisfactory alternative to quitting. There may be some health benefits of smoking fewer cigarettes but there is no evidence to prove it. The only clear benefit is that aiming to reduce use often leads to people eventually stopping.'

⇨ This article first appeared in the Telegraph on 19 July 2007.

Health effects of exposure to secondhand smoke

Information from the United States Environmental Protection Agency

What is secondhand smoke?

Secondhand smoke is a mixture of the smoke given off by the burning end of a cigarette, pipe, or cigar, and the smoke exhaled by smokers. Secondhand smoke is also called environmental tobacco smoke (ETS) and exposure to secondhand smoke is sometimes called involuntary or passive smoking. Secondhand smoke contains more than 4,000 substances, several of which are known to cause cancer in humans or animals.

⇨ EPA has concluded that exposure to secondhand smoke can cause lung cancer in adults who do not smoke. EPA estimates that exposure to secondhand smoke causes approximately 3,000 lung cancer deaths per year in nonsmokers.

⇨ Exposure to secondhand smoke has also been shown in a number of studies to increase the risk of heart disease.

Serious health risks to children

Children are particularly vulnerable to the effects of secondhand smoke because they are still developing physically, have higher breathing rates than adults, and have little control over their indoor environments. Children exposed to high doses of secondhand smoke, such as those whose mothers smoke, run the greatest relative risk of experiencing damaging health effects.

⇨ Exposure to secondhand smoke can cause asthma in children who have not previously exhibited symptoms.

⇨ Exposure to secondhand smoke increases the risk for Sudden Infant Death Syndrome.

⇨ Infants and children younger than 6 who are regularly exposed to secondhand smoke are at increased risk of lower respiratory track infections, such as pneumonia and bronchitis.

⇨ Children who regularly breathe secondhand smoke are at increased risk for middle ear infections.

Health risks to children with asthma:

⇨ Asthma is the most common chronic childhood disease affecting 1 in 13 school-aged children on average.

⇨ Exposure to secondhand smoke can cause new cases of asthma in children who have not previously shown symptoms.

⇨ Exposure to secondhand smoke can trigger asthma attacks and make asthma symptoms more severe.

The science behind the risks

Surgeon general warning: secondhand smoke puts children at risk

On June 27th, 2006, the Surgeon General released a major new report on involuntary exposure to secondhand smoke, concluding that secondhand smoke causes disease and death in children and nonsmoking adults. The report finds a causal relationship between secondhand smoke exposure and Sudden Infant Death Syndrome (SIDS), and declares that the home is becoming the predominant location for exposure of children and adults to secondhand smoke.

The National Survey on Environmental Management of Asthma and Children's Exposure to Environmental Tobacco Smoke (US Environmental Protection Agency, 2004)

Key findings:

⇨ 11% of children aged 6 years and under are exposed to ETS in their homes on a regular basis (4 or more days per week) compared to 20% in the 1998 National Health Interview Survey (NHIS).

⇨ Parents are responsible for 90% of children's exposure to ETS.

⇨ Exposure to ETS is higher and asthma prevalence is more likely in households with low income and low education levels.

⇨ Children with asthma have as much exposure to ETS as children without asthma.

Respiratory Health Effects of Passive Smoking (US Environmental Protection Agency, 1992)

Key findings:

In adults:

⇨ ETS is a human lung carcinogen, responsible for approximately 3,000 lung cancer deaths annually in US nonsmokers. ETS has been classified as a Group A carcinogen under EPA's carcinogen assessment guidelines. This classification is reserved for those compounds or mixtures which have been shown to cause cancer in humans, based on studies in human populations.

In children:

⇨ ETS exposure increases the risk of lower respiratory tract infections such as bronchitis and pneumonia. EPA estimates that between 150,000 and 300,000 of these cases annually in infants and young children up to 18 months of age are attributable to exposure to ETS. Of these, between 7,500 and 15,000 will result in hospitalisation.

⇨ ETS exposure increases the prevalence of fluid in the middle ear, a sign of chronic middle ear disease.

⇨ ETS exposure in children irritates the upper respiratory tract and is associated with a small but significant reduction in lung function.

⇨ ETS exposure increases the frequency of episodes and severity of symptoms in asthmatic children. The report estimates that 200,000 to 1,000,000 asthmatic children have their condition worsened by exposure to environmental tobacco smoke.

⇨ ETS exposure is a risk factor for new cases of asthma in children who have not previously displayed symptoms.

⇨ The above information is reprinted with permission from the US Environmental Protection Agency. Visit www.epa.gov for more information.

© *US Environmental Protection Agency*

Surgeon General's report

US Surgeon General Richard H. Carmona today issued a comprehensive scientific report which concludes that there is no risk-free level of exposure to secondhand smoke. Nonsmokers exposed to secondhand smoke at home or work increase their risk of developing heart disease by 25 to 30 per cent and lung cancer by 20 to 30 per cent. The finding is of major public health concern due to the fact that nearly half of all nonsmoking Americans are still regularly exposed to secondhand smoke.

The report, 'The Health Consequences of Involuntary Exposure to Tobacco Smoke', finds that even brief secondhand smoke exposure can cause immediate harm. The report says the only way to protect nonsmokers from the dangerous chemicals in secondhand smoke is to eliminate smoking indoors.

Secondhand smoke exposure can cause heart disease and lung cancer in nonsmoking adults and is a known cause of sudden infant death syndrome (SIDS), respiratory problems, ear infections, and asthma attacks in infants and children, the report finds.

'The health effects of secondhand smoke exposure are more pervasive than we previously thought,' said Surgeon General Carmona, vice admiral of the US Public Health Service.

'The scientific evidence is now indisputable: secondhand smoke is not a mere annoyance. It is a serious health hazard that can lead to disease and premature death in children and nonsmoking adults.'

Secondhand smoke contains more than 50 cancer-causing chemicals, and is itself a known human carcinogen. Nonsmokers who are exposed to secondhand smoke inhale many of the same toxins as smokers. Even brief exposure to secondhand smoke has immediate adverse effects on the cardiovascular system and increases risk for heart disease and lung cancer, the report says. In addition, the report notes that because the bodies of infants and children are still developing, they are especially vulnerable to the poisons in secondhand smoke.

'The good news is that, unlike some public health hazards, secondhand smoke exposure is easily prevented,' Surgeon General Carmona said.

'Smoke-free indoor environments are proven, simple approaches that prevent exposure and harm.' The report finds that even the most sophisticated ventilation systems cannot completely eliminate secondhand smoke exposure and that only smoke-free environments afford full protection.

⇨ This information was released on 27 June 2006. Visit the US Department of Health and Human Services' website, www.hhs.gov, for more information.

© *US Office of the Surgeon General*

How smoking affects how you look

Information from ASH

Tobacco smoking seriously affects internal organs, particularly the heart and lungs, but it also affects a person's appearance by altering the skin and body weight and shape. While these changes are generally not as life-threatening as heart and lung disease, they can, nevertheless, increase the risk of more serious disorders and have a noticeable ageing effect on the body.

Smoking and the skin

The skin is affected by tobacco smoke in at least two ways. Firstly, tobacco smoke released into the environment has a drying effect on the skin's surface. Secondly, because smoking restricts blood vessels, it reduces the amount of blood flowing to the skin, thus depleting the skin of oxygen and essential nutrients. Some research suggests that smoking may reduce the body's store of Vitamin A, which provides protection against some skin-damaging agents produced by smoking. Another likely explanation is that squinting in response to the irritating nature of the smoke, and the puckering of the mouth when drawing on a cigarette, cause wrinkling around the eyes and mouth.

Skin damaged by smoke has a greyish, wasted appearance. Recent research has shown that the skin-ageing effects of smoking may be due to increased production of an enzyme that breaks down collagen

action on smoking and health

in the skin. Collagen is the main structural protein of the skin which maintains skin elasticity. The more a person smokes, the greater the risk of premature wrinkling. Smokers in their 40s often have as many facial wrinkles as non-smokers in their 60s. In addition to facial wrinkling, smokers may develop hollow cheeks through repeated sucking on cigarettes: this is particularly noticeable in under-weight smokers and can cause smokers to look gaunt. A South Korean study of smokers, non-smokers and ex-smokers aged 20 to 69 found that the current smokers had a higher degree of facial wrinkling than non-smokers and ex-smokers. Past smokers who smoked heavily at a younger age revealed less facial wrinkling than current smokers.

The Chief Medical Officer highlighted the link between smoking and wrinkled, damaged skin, in his 2003 annual report. The report noted that smokers' skin can be prematurely aged by between 10 and 20 years and, although the damaging effects of cigarette smoke on the skin are irreversible, further deterioration can be avoided by stopping smoking.

Prolonged smoking causes discoloration of the fingers and fingernails on the hand used to hold cigarettes. Smoking also results in a yellowing of the teeth and is a cause of halitosis (bad breath).

Smoking and psoriasis

Compared with non-smokers,

smokers have a two to threefold higher risk of developing psoriasis, a chronic skin condition which, while not life-threatening, can be extremely uncomfortable and disfiguring. Some studies have found a dose-response association of smoking and psoriasis, i.e. the risk of the disease increases the longer a person continues to smoke. Smoking also appears to be more strongly associated with psoriasis among women than among men. Smoking may cause as many as one-quarter of all psoriasis cases and may also contribute to as many as half of the cases of palmoplantar pustulosis, a skin disease involving the hands and feet, that some experts view as a form of psoriasis.

Smoking and weight

When people stop smoking, they usually put on weight. Although this is often a cause for concern, the average weight gain is around 2–3kg although this may be temporary. Although the reasons for weight gain are not fully understood, it may be partly explained by the fact that smoking increases the body's metabolic rate – i.e. the rate at which calories are burned up. In addition, nicotine may act as an appetite suppressant so that when smokers quit an increase in appetite leads to an increase in calorie intake. The effect of nicotine on metabolic rate may also explain why smokers tend to weigh less than non-smokers. Experts believe that one way smoking raises metabolic rate is by stimulating the nervous system to produce catecholamines – hormones which cause the heart to beat faster, thus making the body burn more calories. Nicotine also produces more thermogenesis, the process by which the body produces heat. This too, causes the body to use up more calories.

However, a smoking-induced increase in metabolic rate only accounts for about half the difference in weight between the average smoker and average non-smoker. Another likely mechanism is that smoking alters the body-weight set point, i.e. the weight towards which a person tends to return despite attempts to gain or lose weight. Smoking appears to lower a person's normal weight and the weight gained on stopping reflects a return to the body's natural weight set point.

Women and girls tend to be more concerned about their weight and body shape than men, and weight control may be influential in causing the higher incidence of smoking among teenage girls. However, post-cessation weight gain can be modified by eating a low-fat, calorie-reduced diet and by moderately increased exercise. One study found that stopping smoking resulted in a net excess weight gain of about 2.4kg in middle-aged women but that among those women who increased physical activity after stopping smoking, weight gain was between 1.3kg and 1.8kg.

While weight gain is common immediately after stopping smoking, in the longer term, ex-smokers weight may return to the comparative weight of someone who has never smoked. A Japanese study examined the relationship between weight gain and the length of time after stopping smoking. Researchers found that although heavy smokers experienced large weight gain and weighed more than never smokers in the few years after smoking cessation, thereafter they lost weight to the never smoker level. Among former light and moderate smokers, weight was gained up to the never–smoker level but without any further excess gain.

Body shape

Although smokers tend to be thinner than non-smokers, the effect of smoking on the endocrine system (glands which secrete hormones) causes smokers to store even normal amounts of body fat in an abnormal distribution. Smokers are more likely to store fat around the waist and upper torso, rather than around the hips. This means smokers are more

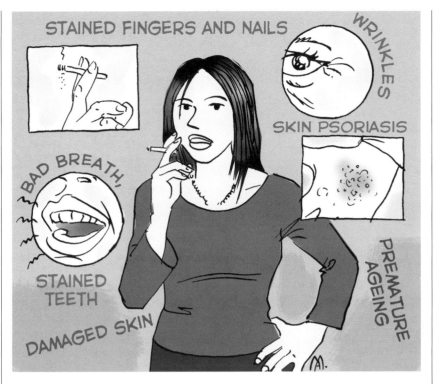

likely to have a higher waist-to-hip ratio (WHR) than non-smokers. A high WHR is associated with a much higher risk of developing diabetes, heart disease, high blood pressure, gallbladder problems and (in women) cancer of the womb and breast. In one study of nearly 12,000 pre- and postmenopausal women aged 40 to 73, the waist to hip ratio increased as the number of cigarettes smoked per day increased. A study of American men also found a dose-response relationship between the number of cigarettes smoked and waist-to-hip ratio.

However, changes to WHR induced by smoking need not be permanent. A Swedish study examined the effect of smoking

and smoking cessation on the distribution of fat in a representative sample of women. The study found that women who stopped smoking experienced less upper-body fat deposition than would be expected by their accompanying weight gain. This suggests that while some weight gain after stopping smoking can be expected, it is less of a health risk because it is not deposited in the upper torso, where it is associated with increased risk of heart disease.

⇨ This information is reprinted with permission from ASH (Action on Smoking and Health). Visit www.ash.org.uk for more information.

© ASH 2007

Pregnancy and smoking

By Dr Phillip Owen, consultant obstetrician and gynaecologist

Pregnancy is about creating a new life, but ultimately it is the mother's decision whether or not to continue smoking. Your pregnancy can be a powerful motivation to give up smoking, because you're making this choice on behalf of your unborn child who is completely dependent on you.

Pre-pregnancy

Smoking makes it harder to conceive, irrespective of which partner smokes.

Both female and male smokers have lower fertility levels, while adults who were born to mothers who smoked have less chance of becoming a parent themselves. Smoking also reduces the chances of IVF succeeding.

It's thought nicotine reduces a woman's fertility by affecting the production of hormones that are necessary for pregnancy. Smoking also impedes the transportation of the egg through the Fallopian tubes to the womb.

Male smokers tend to have a sperm count that is 15 per cent lower than that of non-smokers. Smoking can also:
- reduce the amount of semen;
- harm the motility of sperm, i.e. their ability to move around;
- affect their shape.

Smoking can also affect the blood vessels that supply the penis, causing erection problems.

If you're trying for a baby, all of the above could impair fertility.

Quitting smoking will increase your ability to conceive and your likelihood of success with IVF.

Why is it harmful to smoke during pregnancy?

A baby in the womb gets everything from its mother. Nutrients and oxygen come via the placenta and umbilical cord. Smoking not only exposes the foetus to toxins in tobacco smoke, but it also damages placental function.

When a person smokes, some of the oxygen in their blood is replaced by carbon monoxide. If a pregnant woman smokes, her blood and therefore her child's blood will contain less oxygen than normal. This can cause the foetal heart rate to rise as baby struggles to get enough oxygen.

The particles in tobacco smoke contain different toxic substances that change the blood's ability to work in a healthy and normal manner. This can affect the placenta that feeds the baby.

How smoking harms the unborn baby

Babies born to mothers who smoke:
- are more likely to be born prematurely and with a low birth weight (below 2.5kg or 5lb 8oz).
- have a birth weight on average 200g (7oz) less than those born to non-smokers. This effect increases proportionally – the more the mother smokes, the less the child weighs.
- have organs that are smaller on average than babies born to non-smokers.
- have poorer lung function.
- are twice as likely to die from cot death. There seems to be a direct link between cot death and parents smoking.
- are ill more frequently. Babies born to women who smoked 15 cigarettes or more a day during pregnancy are taken into hospital twice as often during the first eight months of life.
- get painful diseases such as inflammation of the middle ear and asthmatic bronchitis more frequently in early childhood.
- are more likely to become smokers themselves in later years.

In addition, pregnant women who smoke increase their risk of early miscarriage.

In later pregnancy, smoking mothers are at increased risk of the baby's placenta coming away from the womb before the baby is born (placental abruption). This may cause the baby to be born prematurely, starve of oxygen, or even to die in the womb (stillborn).

I'm pregnant and still smoking

It is never too late to stop smoking. Every cigarette you decide not to smoke will help your and baby's health.

Much of the damage caused by smoking can be reversed because your body is a living organism that has the ability to heal itself.

Women who stopped smoking at the halfway point in their pregnancy gave birth to babies with the same average weight as women who had not smoked at all during pregnancy.

You may be tempted just to cut down, but many smokers find they inhale more deeply when smoking fewer cigarettes. So though the number of cigarettes decreases, the intake of damaging substances doesn't because residues are concentrated towards the butt.

Other studies show that even moderate cigarette smoking is damaging to the foetus, making quitting the most important thing you can do to improve your and baby's health.

How to stop smoking

You can get support and advice about stopping smoking from your midwife, antenatal clinic or GP. Evidence shows that counselling by qualified health professionals can double quit rates for pregnant women.

Nicotine replacement therapy (NRT) should not ideally be used by pregnant women as an aid to stopping smoking. But for the heaviest smokers who are unable to give up using willpower alone, NRT will deliver less nicotine than cigarettes and none of the other disease-causing agents, e.g. tar.

You should only use NRT while pregnant after carefully discussing all the risks and benefits with your doctor.

⇨ The above information is reprinted with permission from NetDoctor. Visit www.netdoctor.co.uk for more information.

©NetDoctor

Babies born to smoking mothers

In the latest of a series of interviews from the Royal Economic Society Conference 2007, Romesh Vaitilingam talks to Emma Tominey about the effect of smoking during pregnancy

Mothers who smoke during pregnancy will have smaller babies. But much of the harm is due to unobservable traits of the mother. If mums stub it out by the time they are five months pregnant, the damage is as good as undone.

At the same time, the lasting harm to babies is greatest if the mothers have low education. So a much more holistic approach to improving child health in pregnancy is needed to help thousands of children break out of the poverty trap.

These are the conclusions of extensive new research by Emma Tominey, presented to the Royal Economic Society's 2007 annual conference at the University of Warwick, 11–13 April.

Babies born to women who smoke will typically be 5.4% (6.5oz) lighter than other babies. But around half of this damage is because of unobservable traits of the mother. This means that stopping mothers smoking during pregnancy is important, but it is only half of the battle.

So while the effects of being a small baby stay with a child throughout its life, affecting its health, education and earnings potential, stopping a mother from smoking must be combined with helping her to be healthier in other areas of her life.

But for the harm that remains, the low educated mothers are hardest hit. Children born to mothers who left school at the age of 16 suffer double the harm for each cigarette smoked. The government must target its policy directly at these low educated families.

Women who do smoke in the early stages of pregnancy should not be 'written off' as 'too late'. Surprisingly, the research shows that the harm to the baby is essentially reduced to zero if the mother quits by month five of the pregnancy.

This is much longer than conventional wisdom and previous research has suggested and tells us there's more time than we thought to help the mothers change their behaviour during pregnancy.

The study is based on research into the lives of 6,500 children and their mothers, and went into exceptional detail of the mother's lifestyle over her lifetime. The mothers were tracked from their child's birth until the age of 42.

The research suggests that while previous studies have identified a link between smoking and low birth weight, none has looked in such depth at whether the experiences of the mother can alter this and how the harm accumulates during pregnancy.

The study calls on the government to alter radically its policy on helping pregnant women quit smoking, developing a more holistic approach to improving the health of these children during pregnancy and targeting the children of low educated mothers.

⇨ The above information is reprinted with permission from the Royal Economic Society. Visit whystudyeconomics.ac.uk for more information.

© Royal Economic Society

Lung cancer

Frequently asked questions

Q. What causes lung cancer?

A. The vast majority – over 80% – of lung cancers are caused by smoking tobacco or by indirect exposure to tobacco smoke (passive smoking). The other main causes are breathing industrial chemicals such as asbestos, arsenic and polycyclic hydrocarbons or the natural radioactive gas, radon.

Q. Who is at risk?

A. Like most cancers, the risk of lung cancer increases with age. The longer you smoke, the greater your risk. Very few cases are diagnosed in people under 40 and the most common age of diagnosis is between 70 and 74. In the US 91,000 men and 79,000 women are diagnosed with lung cancer each year. In the UK the figures are 23,000 men and 15,000 women.

Q. Does lung cancer run in families?

A. There are very few, if any, inherited conditions that increase the risk of lung cancer in non-smokers. However, not all of the people who smoke get lung cancer and there may be an inherited component which influences whether or not smoking will cause lung cancer.

Q. Does diet affect the risk of getting lung cancer?

A. This is still being investigated, but research to date has not found any link between diet and lung cancer.

Q. Are there different types of lung cancer?

A. There are four main types of lung cancer: small cell lung cancer, squamous cell carcinoma, large cell carcinoma and adenocarcinoma. Tobacco smoking is strongly linked to the first three but only weakly linked to adenocarcinoma. However, this type of lung cancer has been linked to the use of low-tar cigarettes.

Q. What are the symptoms of lung cancer?

A. There are a variety of symptoms of lung cancer, including difficulty breathing, coughing up blood, chest pain, loss of appetite, weight loss and general fatigue. Some lung cancers do not cause any noticeable symptoms until they are quite advanced and have spread to other parts of the body.

Q. How is lung cancer diagnosed?

A. Lung cancers are sometimes first detected on routine chest X-rays. However, the main method of diagnosis is bronchoscopy, in which a thin, flexible tube is inserted down the airways (under anaesthetic), allowing doctors to see the inside of the lungs and even take a biopsy (a sample small of the suspect tissue). A CT scan, liver ultrasound or bone scan may also be used to find out if the cancer has spread.

Q. How is lung cancer treated?

A. Drug treatment (chemotherapy) is the usual treatment for small cell lung cancers, because they usually spread too quickly for surgery to be useful. Radiotherapy is also often used. For the other types of lung cancer, surgery is first used to remove the main tumour, if it has not spread too far. If surgery is not possible, then radiotherapy is used instead. Depending on the type of tumour and how advanced it is, chemotherapy can be used in different ways: either to shrink the tumour before surgery or after surgery to kill off any remaining cancer cells.

Q. How effective is the treatment?

A. Lung cancer is one of the most dangerous cancers. The available treatments can prolong the patient's life, but complete cures are very rare. Four out of every five lung cancer patients die within one year of being diagnosed. Only one in twenty is alive five years after diagnosis. Many of these are people diagnosed with early squamous cell carcinomas, which can be treated successfully by surgical removal.

Q. What are the side effects of treatment?

A. The drug treatments cause bruising, fatigue, hair loss, diarrhoea, nausea and vomiting. However, the nausea and vomiting can now be reduced or even eliminated by special drugs. The hair loss may be partial or complete, but it is always temporary. The hair will grow back.

⇨ The above information is reprinted with permission from the Association for International Cancer Research. Visit www.aicr.org.uk for more information.

© *Association for International Cancer Research*

How to kick the habit

Information from YouthNet

Sometimes it can seem like everyone smokes, which can make it tempting to be part of the pack. Kicking the habit takes guts, but it's also the greatest thing you'll ever do for your body. Stay smoke-free and you can be sure you'll be proud of your achievement.

Burning truths

➪ Tobacco in cigarettes contains a highly addictive drug called nicotine.

➪ Nicotine is actually a stimulant – smoking speeds up the body system increasing your heart rate and blood pressure.

➪ There are more than 4000 chemicals in tobacco, most of which are bad for your health

➪ Smoking can leave your skin up to 40% thinner than normal, making early wrinkles all part of the package.

➪ Every day people give up smoking in a way that works for them. Some go for hypnosis or nicotine patches, but ultimately it takes willpower.

You've got to want to quit

➪ Make a date to stop smoking and stick to it.

➪ Steer clear of smoke–situations.

➪ Don't look for an excuse to light up. Chewing gum can help keep the craving at bay (anything that keeps your mouth or hands occupied).

➪ At moments of weakness focus on the plus points: Save cash. Feel better. Smell fresher. Live longer.

➪ If you turn to the fridge instead of the fags, make sure it's stocked with healthy food so you don't have to worry about your waistline.

➪ Remember that every day you go without a smoke you're beating the addiction.

After you quit:

➪ 20 mins – your blood pressure drops back to normal levels.

➪ Two days – there's no more nicotine left in your body.

➪ Three to nine months – your lung capacity improves by 10%.

➪ Five months – your risk of a heart attack is 50% less than a smoker.

➪ 10 years – your chances of a heart attack falls to the same as someone who has never lit up.

Save money

➪ A pack of fags costs around a fiver.

➪ Stub out a 20–a–day habit and save well over a grand in a year.

Save your life

Smoke and your chances of dying early will shoot up. Here's what a long–term habit can do:

➪ Cancer (lungs, mouth, nose, throat, leukaemia).

➪ Chronic breathing problems like bronchitis and emphysema.

➪ Coronary heart disease, strokes and even gangrene.

➪ The above information is reprinted with permission from YouthNet. Visit www.thesite.org for more information.

©YouthNet

Craving a smoke? Take a walk instead

Information from the American Cancer Society

People who are trying to quit smoking should take a quick walk when they feel like lighting up, British researchers say. In a recent review of studies, they found that even a few minutes of physical activity can help reduce cigarette cravings and withdrawal symptoms.

The team from the University of Exeter looked at 14 studies that examined the effect of exercise on cigarette cravings, withdrawal symptoms, mood, or smoking behaviour among smokers who were trying to quit, either permanently or temporarily. Their results were published in a recent issue of the journal *Addiction*.

Exercise significantly reduced cigarette cravings, they found, even when it was a low-intensity activity like isometrics (a type of strength training that involves pushing or pulling against an immovable object) or stretching, and even when people did only 5 minutes of activity.

Longer periods of more intense exercise – a brisk 15-minute walk, for instance – held cravings at bay for as long as 50 minutes. Exercise also helped lessen the severity of withdrawal symptoms including stress, anxiety, tension, poor concentration, irritability, and restlessness.

Lead researcher Adrian Taylor, PhD, says exercise could be an alternative to snacking for many smokers who are trying to quit, especially since the amount of time and activity required to cut cravings is minimal.

'People tend to think of exercise as a visit to the gym, or requiring the need to put on specific clothing, or to be done on a set number of days a week, or only possible on weekends when time is less of a problem,' but that is not necessarily true, says Taylor, an associate professor

in exercise and health psychology at Exeter.

The key is simply to do something active when the urge to smoke strikes. 'If it takes an average of 6 minutes to smoke a cigarette, then doing a brisk walk for this period may be sufficient to help remove the urge,' he says. Doctors should encourage their patients to use exercise as a tool when they're trying to quit smoking, he adds.

'General practitioners should be asking patients to

think about the times and situations they really want a cigarette and advise them to seek to incorporate short bouts of exercise around these,' says Taylor.

Tom Glynn, PhD, director of cancer science and trends and director of international tobacco programmes for the American Cancer Society, agrees that exercise should be a part of every smoker's quitting plan. But it shouldn't be the only quitting tool doctors and patients discuss, he cautions.

Several types of cessation aids have been shown to help smokers quit, including nicotine replacement therapy, antidepressants and other medications, and counselling.

To date, no studies have compared exercise to medications in terms of their effectiveness at helping smokers quit, but Taylor says his study suggests they are comparable methods. And new tools are always needed.

'What we do know is that success rates for quitting (after 1 year) using even the best aids and support available are not much more than 25%, so there is scope for finding new aids,' he says.

And for smokers who cannot take medication, exercise is an especially realistic and valuable option, he points out.

'Giving a quitter an understanding of the options available – and exercise is now clearly one – is important,' Taylor says. 'Exercise has many other benefits and no side effects. It needs to be promoted as a cheap and convenient, serious option as a smoking cessation aid.'

⇨ This information is reprinted with permission from the American Cancer Society, Inc. Visit www.cancer.org for more information.
© *US American Cancer Society*

Nicotine replacement

Information from YouthNet

People smoke for the nicotine hit, not for the damage it does to their health. Nicotine replacement therapy (NRT) is a way of delivering the same kind of hit, while cutting out the tar and other poisonous chemicals.

Is there a catch?

Nicotine raises blood pressure, which means pregnant women, nursing mothers or anyone suffering from circulation problems should avoid any form of NRT. Also be sure to follow the manufacturer instructions and never exceed the recommended use. Otherwise you could end up boosting your nicotine intake, and making your bid to quit even harder!

Where can I get hold of it?

Most forms of NRT are available from chemists, but you have to be 18 or over before you can give it a try. Clinically proven to help reduce the number of cigarettes smoked, NRT is available in a number of different forms:

Nicotine patches

They look like sticking plasters, and serve to heal your nicotine craving. Each one contains a small amount of the drug, which is absorbed steadily and slowly through the skin. As a result it's not going to help you beat a sudden craving, but it should help take the edge off the whole withdrawal process.
⇨ Generally, one nicotine patch lasts either 16 or 24 hours.
⇨ Experts recommend a three-month course for maximum effectiveness.
⇨ At the same time, aim to reduce the rate at which you get through patches.

Nicotine gum

NRT gum is most effective at beating off any sudden desire to spark up. The hit is faster-acting than patches, as the nicotine is released through the mouth and swiftly absorbed into the bloodstream.
⇨ NRT chewy is available in different strengths.
⇨ Experts recommend chewing through no more than 10–15 pieces a day, and then slowly cutting out the habit over a period of three months.
⇨ Go easy on the gum — over-zealous chewing lead to feelings of nausea or dizziness.

Nicotine inhalator

An appealing method if you miss the cigarette as much as the smoking. Nicotine inhalators are plastic, and look like cigarette holders. A nicotine capsule can be fitted inside, which releases a hit whenever you inhale on the mouthpiece.
⇨ Nicotine inhalators deliver a tenth of the nicotine you get from a hit on a cigarette.
⇨ Many users are drawn to the inhalator because they miss having a ciggie in their hand.
⇨ It is advisable to use no more than 15 cartridges a day, and gradually withdraw over a three-month period. If in doubt, see your GP.

Nicotine nasal spray

A squirt of this stuff into your nostril is a fast and effective way of satisfying a craving. It basically releases a spray of nicotine, and this is absorbed through the membranes inside your nose.
⇨ NRT nasal spray is only available on prescription.
⇨ Experts recommend spraying about 10–15 times each day, and then easing off over a three month period.
⇨ Some users have reported side effects such as a peppery sensation at the back of the throat, along with some coughing and sneezing.

⇨ The above information is reprinted with permission from YouthNet. Visit www.thesite.org for more information.

©YouthNet

Smoking, giving up and mental health

Information from Mind

While general smoking rates are falling, this is not the case amongst the psychiatric populations, who suffer poor health as a consequence.

Smoking rates for people from this group tend to be, on average, twice as high as those for the general public. Smokers with a mental health problem also tend to smoke more heavily and be more dependent than smokers without mental health problems. For example, 51 per cent of individuals with a schizophrenia diagnosis and 50 per cent of those with a bipolar affective disorder smoked over 20 cigarettes a day compared to only eight per cent of the general population. A US survey estimated that in one particular month, 45 per cent of all the cigarettes smoked were consumed by individuals with a psychiatric or substance misuse disorder.

Smoking-related fatal diseases are also more prominent among individuals experiencing mental health problems than amongst the general public. A study in Finland found that having a mental health disorder predicted a higher risk of cardiovascular disease, coronary heart disease and respiratory disease. It also found that individuals with schizophrenia were almost ten times more at risk of dying of a respiratory disease than other participants. These people are also often the least capable of coping with the effects of devastating medical illnesses caused by smoking.

It was found that smoking, in contradiction to popular belief, exacerbates stress, anxiety and sleep disorders. All of these are detrimental to most mental health conditions. Anxiety levels fall significantly after successfully giving up smoking for one week.

A research review found that smokers reported above-average stress prior to smoking, rather than below-average stress after smoking. Smokers smoke mainly to avoid the stress that nicotine depletion causes.

Financial impact

Smokers with a mental health problem can spend a large percentage of their, often low, income on tobacco and cigarettes. In a US study it was estimated that a smoker with schizophrenia spends just over one-third of their weekly income on cigarettes. This money is therefore not available to be spent on food, heating, socialising or other things such as leisure activities which could help to improve quality of life. As a consequence, physical and mental health might suffer.

Interestingly, one of the reasons for smoking, stated by McNeill, is that it is a coping mechanism to deal with the stress of financial hardship. This is obviously a perception from the smoker, just as stress reduction is only a perceived benefit.

Impact of the smoking ban

Socially the ban might lead to isolation of individuals who are heavy smokers; they may find it difficult to go out because they are no longer allowed to smoke in the places where they go to socialise, such as cafés or drop-in centres. Some may feel stigmatised as smokers because of increased emphasis on the negative effects of smoking in the media, and because in order to smoke they will have to go outside and be seen by the world as smokers. It could also lead to increased isolation if people are more inclined to stay home where they can smoke out of view.

For some people with mental health problems, simply attending an appointment with a health professional can be a source of anxiety. Not being able to smoke in the building while waiting to be seen could result in additional stress, which might be reflected in increased numbers of missed appointments.

On a positive note, it might give people an opportunity to give up or at

---

Smoking near others

Non-smokers' reasons for saying that they would mind if smokers smoked near them[1], 2005, Great Britain

Reason	Percentage
Bad for my health	46%
Affects breathing/asthma	25%
Makes me cough	18%
Gets in my eyes	18%
Makes me feel sick	10%
Gives me a headache	7%
Unpleasant smell	64%
Makes clothes smell	50%
Other	13%

Health reasons
Other reasons

percentage[2]

1. Adults aged 16 and over.
2. Percentages add up to more than 100% because some people gave more than one reason.

Source: Smoking-Related Behaviour and Attitudes, 2005. Office for National Statistics. Crown copyright.

---

least to examine their smoking – one of the most difficult things people giving up report is not smoking in social situations, especially in pubs and cafés.

The smoking ban will also have a big impact on professionals. It has been found that interventions and policies around smoking are less popular among mental health staff than other healthcare professionals. A small-scale UK study found that female mental health nurses smoked twice as much as non-mental health nurses. The ban will mean that this group of people cannot smoke while working any more. It will also mean a change in culture: anecdotal evidence indicates that some mental health staff use smoking as 'a way of social interaction and to facilitate communication'. A new way of working and relating will have to be found by these staff.

On the other hand it may also make their job healthier, and for those staff who smoke it might be seen as an opportunity to try to give up smoking. Perhaps giving up smoking together with clients will give fresh opportunities for building therapeutic relationships.

The voluntary sector will have to go smoke-free as well. This will put some initial strain on staff implementing the policy and working with service users around it. But it is also an opportunity; for example, Mind Aberystwyth, a therapeutic service in Wales, has been smoke-free from the day they opened in 2005. In that same year they developed a smoking cessation service. This service has recorded good results and members are happy that the premises are smoke-free. Even the smokers comment positively on how it reduces their smoking because they have to go outside to light up. It also offers staff an opportunity to talk about smoking behaviour with members, examining possibilities of giving up.

⇨ This information is reprinted from *Smoking, giving up and mental health* with permission from Mind (National Association for Mental Health). Visit www.mind.org.uk for more information.

© 2007 Mind

⇨ Around 10 million adults smoke cigarettes in Great Britain. This is about a quarter of the population: 25% of men and 23% of women. (page 1)

⇨ The proportion of children who have experimented with smoking has fallen from 53% in 1982 to 39% in 2004. (page 2)

⇨ Since 1993, girls have been more likely than boys to have ever smoked. (page 2)

⇨ Europe has the highest incidence of teen smokers in the world. (page 4)

⇨ Images young people see of those who smoke, drink or take drugs, have greater impact on their behaviour than anything others may say to them. (page 6)

⇨ An EU-wide ban on advertising tobacco products came into force in August 2005. (page 7)

⇨ A study in California found that there are now about 11 depictions of smoking in every hour of the typical film. (page 8)

⇨ Studies in different countries show a correlation between the amount of smoking imagery in films and the likelihood of young teenagers starting to smoke. (page 9)

⇨ In July 2007, enclosed public places in England became smokefree. (page 11)

⇨ Irish cigarette sales fell by around 17% following a public smoking ban. (page 12)

⇨ Owners and managers of pubs, clubs and cafes face fines of up to £2,500 if they allow customers to smoke on their premises. (page 12)

⇨ The vast majority of Londoners (83%) support the Government's ban on smoking in public places. (page 13)

⇨ Sales of cheap cigarettes are growing while sales in the premium category are falling. (page 16)

⇨ Fewer people in professional jobs smoke compared with people in manual and routine work. (page 21)

⇨ Tobacco consumption has fallen over the past 20 years in most high-income countries, but is expected to increase in developing countries. (page 22)

⇨ In 2002 the world's three largest tobacco multinationals had combined tobacco revenues greater than the total combined GDP of 27 developing countries. (page 22)

⇨ By 2030, a projected 7 million people in developing countries will be killed every year by tobacco. (page 23)

⇨ Asthma is the most common chronic childhood disease affecting 1 in 13 school-aged children on average. (page 28)

⇨ Exposure to environmental tobacco smoke is higher and asthma prevalence is more likely in households with low income and low education levels. (page 29)

⇨ In children, environmental tobacco smoke exposure increases the risk of lower respiratory tract infections such as bronchitis and pneumonia. (page 29)

⇨ A South Korean study of smokers, non-smokers and ex-smokers aged 20 to 69 found that the current smokers had a higher degree of facial wrinkling than non-smokers and ex-smokers. (page 30)

⇨ Smokers are more likely to store fat around the waist and upper torso, rather than around the hips. (page 31)

⇨ Male smokers tend to have a sperm count that is 15 per cent lower than that of non-smokers.. (page 32)

⇨ Babies born to mothers who smoke are more likely to be born prematurely and with a low birth weight. (page 32)

⇨ There seems to be a direct link between cot death and parents smoking. (page 32)

⇨ Women who stopped smoking at the halfway point in their pregnancy gave birth to babies with the same average weight as women who had not smoked at all during pregnancy. (page 33)

⇨ Children born to mothers who left school at the age of 16 suffer double the harm for each cigarette smoked. (page 33)

⇨ Over 80% of lung cancers are caused by smoking tobacco directly, or passive smoking. (page 34)

⇨ Physical activity can help reduce cigarette cravings and withdrawal symptoms. (page 36)

⇨ Nicotine replacement therapy delivers a nicotine hit while cutting out the tar and other poisonous chemicals. (page 37)

⇨ Smoking rates for people with mental health problems tend to be, on average, twice as high as those for the general public. (page 38)

GLOSSARY

Abstinence
Refraining from doing something by choice.

Acrolein
A chemical produced when glycerine burns that can cause irritation, found in tobacco smoke.

Arsenic
A poisonous metallic element, found in tobacco smoke.

Benzene
A carcinogenic, aromatic compound, found in tobacco smoke.

Carbon monoxide
A toxic gas released when something is burnt incompletely, found in tobacco smoke.

Carcinogen
Any substance that is known to cause cancer.

Cash crop
A crop grown for sale, not for local consumption.

Compliance
Conforming with laws and regulations.

Cot death
More commonly known as sudden infant death syndrome, it is the sudden and unexpected death of an apparently healthy baby during sleep.

Cyanide
A poisonous compound, found in tobacco smoke.

Developing countries
Countries with a low per capita income, generally associated with poverty.

Formaldehyde
A strong-smelling and irritating gas, found in tobacco smoke.

GDP
Gross domestic product (GDP) is the value of all goods and services produced in a country in a year.

Initiation
Starting something for the first time.

Metabolise
To be broken down into energy by the body's cells.

Nicotine dependence
Compulsion to smoke cigarettes to avoid feeling bad.

Passive smoking
Breathing in air polluted with other people's smoking.

Smoking cessation
To quit smoking.

Smoking prevalence
The number or percentage of people in a population that smoke at a given time.

Snuff
Powdered tobacco, inhaled through the nose.

Tobacco duty
An abbreviation of tobacco products duty, it is a type of tax charged on purchases of tobacco products.

Tobacco sponsorship
When tobacco companies give money to other companies to have their brand name associated with a product.

Toluene
A toxic and aromatic compound, found in tobacco smoke.

Withdrawal
The physical and psychological symptoms that appear when someone dependent on a substance stops using it.

INDEX

Additional Resources

Other Issues *titles*
If you are interested in researching further some of the issues raised in *Smoking Trends*, you may like to read the following titles in the **Issues** series:

⇨ Vol. 143 *Problem Drinking*
(ISBN 9781 86168 409 7)
⇨ Vol. 128 *The Cannabis Issue*
(ISBN 9781 86168 374 8)
⇨ Vol. 123 *Young People and Health*
(ISBN 9781 86168 362 5)
⇨ Vol. 114 *Drug Abuse*
(ISBN 9781 86168 347 2)

For more information about these titles, visit our website at www.independence.co.uk/publicationslist

Useful organisations
You may find the websites of the following organisations useful for further research:

⇨ ASH (Action on Smoking and Health): www.ash.org.uk

⇨ Association for International Cancer Research: www.aicr.org.uk

⇨ Cancer Research UK: www.cancerresearchuk.org

⇨ NHS Quit Smoking Service for Enfield and Haringey: www.quitsmoking.uk.com

ACKNOWLEDGEMENTS

The publisher is grateful for permission to reproduce the following material.

While every care has been taken to trace and acknowledge copyright, the publisher tenders its apology for any accidental infringement or where copyright has proved untraceable. The publisher would be pleased to come to a suitable arrangement in any such case with the rightful owner.

Chapter One: Smoking and Society

Smoking statistics, © ASH, Young people and smoking, © ASH, Europe 'worst' for teen smoking, © Agence France Presse, What's the effect of peer pressure on smoking?, © Crown copyright, Why the young smoke and how to stop them, © Economic and Social Research Council, How images affect young people's own lifestyles, © Economic and Social Research Council, EU advertising ban, © biz/ed, Hollywood faces fury as smoking on screen returns to 1950s levels, © Telegraph Group Limited, Smoking in movies linked to increase in global youth smoking, © ASH, Smoking regulations in England, © Crown copyright, Smoking ban 'to save 500,000 lives', © Press Association, Potential increase in pub patronage after ban, © Ipsos MORI, Attitudes of Londoners to the public smoking ban, © Ipsos MORI, Third of bosses to axe cigarette breaks, © Associated Newspapers Ltd, Legal challenge to smoking ban, © Press Association, Smoking ban can seriously damage your brand, © Telegraph Group Limited, Hundreds complain about anti-smoking ads, © National News, Ten-pack ban may cut teen smoking, © Telegraph Group Limited, Young people and nicotine patches, © NCJ Media Limited, National smoking map shows poverty link, © Cancer Research UK, Tobacco in the developing world, © ASH, Smoking in developing countries, © Cancer Research UK

Chapter Two: Smoking and Health

How nicotine works, © HowStuffWorks.com, Benefits timeline, © NHS Quit Smoking Service for Enfield and Haringey, Smoking less 'is no healthier', © Telegraph Group Limited, Health effects of exposure to secondhand smoke, © US Environmental Protection Agency, Surgeon General's report, © US Office of the Surgeon General, How smoking affects how you look, © ASH, Pregnancy and smoking, © NetDoctor, Babies born to smoking mothers, © Royal Economic Society, Lung cancer, © Association for International Cancer Research, How to kick the habit, © YouthNet, Craving a smoke? Take a walk instead, © US American Cancer Society, Nicotine replacement, © YouthNet, Smoking, giving up and mental health, © 2007 Mind

Illustrations and photographs

P1: Krisztian Pinter; p2: Kasper Nowak; p5; Angelo Madrid; p7: Ben and Kaz Askins; p8: Simon Kneebone; p10: Don Hatcher; p11: Josep Altarriba; p12: Barney Livingston; p13: Don Hatcher; p14; Bev Aisbett; p17: Simon Kneebone; p19: Matt Redmond; p20: Cobi Smith; p23: Silvia Cosimini; p24: Wen-Yan King; p25: Simon Kneebone; p28 and 31: Angelo Madrid; p34: Rodrigo Matias; p35: Don Hatcher; p37: Simon Kneebone; p39: Don Hatcher.

Graphs

All graphs by Lisa Firth.

And with thanks to the team: Mary Chapman, Sandra Dennis and Jan Haskell.

Cobi Smith and Sophie Crewdson
Cambridge
September, 2007